COMPLETE GUIDE TO ★ 3-GUN COMPETITION

BY CHAD ADAMS

Published by

Gun Digest® Books, an imprint of F+W Media, Inc.
Krause Publications • 700 East State Street • Iola, WI 54990-0001
715-445-2214 • 888-457-2873
www.krausebooks.com

To order books or other products call toll-free 1-800-258-0929
or visit us online at www.gundigeststore.com

Cover photography by
Yamil R. Sued/Photoworks, www.hotgunshots.com

All photos by 3-Gun Nation, except where indicated by Yamil R. Sued.

ISBN-13: 978-1-4402-3648-8
ISBN-10: 1-4402-3648-8

Cover Design by Dave Hauser
Designed by Dave Hauser
Edited by Jennifer L.S. Pearsall

Printed in United States of America

Acknowledgements

There are a tremendous number of folks to thank who have made this work possible. 3-gunners Patrick Kelley, Bryan Ray, Bruce Piatt, Rob Romero, Jansen Jones, Mike Voigt, Tommy Thacker, Taran Butler, Tony Holmes, and many more have patiently fielded my calls, returned my e-mails, and more. Match directors Dan Furbee, Andy Horner, JJ and Denise Johnson, Ken Flood, Mike, Rhonda and Travis Gibson and Tenille (Gibson) Chidester at MGM Ironman, Larry Houck, Sheldon Carruth, Kirk Broyles, Gary Welborn, and more have given me and my company access, explained their match design philosophy, and been instrumental in the success of 3GN thus far. A special thanks to NRA Board Member Joe DeBergalis, our patron saint of 3-Gun.

FNH USA's Ken Pfau and Tommy Thacker have been more than influential, and I am one among many who thanks them for providing sponsorship, support staff, knowledge, and even gear for our Tour. Federal Premium, Stag Arms, Cheaper Than Dirt, NSSF, Brownells, DoubleStar, Samson Manufacturing, Timney Triggers, Ruger, MGM Targets, SureFire, Leupold Tactical Opticsand many others also deserve much credit for their contributions. I, we, thank you one and all.

TABLE OF Contents

Intro

3-Gun Nation means a lot of things to a lot of different people in the sport of 3-gun. For some, it's on the periphery of what they do, while others plan their entire shooting careers around the programs and competitive platforms developed by 3-Gun Nation (3GN). Regardless the level of one's involvement, since the debut of 3GN, in 2010, it's hard to argue the dynamic explosion in the popularity of what we like to call the "X-Games of the Shooting Sports."

I discovered 3-gun through my profession, which makes me unique. Most folks' jobs simply don't enable them to go out and try new shooting sports with little financial investment or effort. So, I was lucky, because mine did. However, had I not had such amazing access to the firearms industry, I'm not sure if I ever would have found what has become my passion.

On a fundamental level, I think there's something wrong with that.

I happened to grow up in small-town America, where there wasn't any particular interest, at least to my knowledge, in action shooting. Guns were for hunting, or for defense, or even simply for setting up tin cans and having fun. Football and basketball were sports—real competition. My view of shooting while I was growing up really didn't equate the cool black and tactical guns I liked with any type of "sport" I knew anything about.

So that's the real purpose of this book—an attempt to educate folks, potentially like me, who are not acutely aware of what 3-gun is and how they can get involved. My job has enabled me to get to know the top shooters in the sport, and many of them have helped me along the way, teaching me what I, as a journalist, should be writing about, and how to relay that knowledge to newer shooters. This book is an attempt to take what I've learned from the sport of 3-gun and package it into something useful for anyone interested in playing the game.

This book is for anyone interested in 3-gun, for the top shooters who have driven the sport, for the companies that support it, and for the next great stars of the game, the guys like Rustin Bernskoetter who are out there competing with a philosophy of "shoot until my fingers bleed," as he says. I hope you'll enjoy what's in the pages of this book and come join us in this exploding sport. We're truly looking forward to seeing you on the range.

— *Chad Adams*

3-GUN 101:

An Introduction to America's Fastest Growing Shooting Sport

The sport of 3-gun falls within the discipline known as "action shooting," which really is a politically correct term for *practical* shooting, the sport based on the quest for a higher level of *combat* shooting. While action shooting has been formally presented in America now for several decades, it has taken various shapes.

Today, action shooting has many forms, most of which traces itself back to the formation of the International Practical Shooting Confederation, or IPSC. Later, the United States Practical Shooting Association was formed as the U.S. domain of IPSC, as IPSC is truly international and branches into many countries around the world. The USPSA remains the strongest region, boasting more than 20,000 members nationwide.

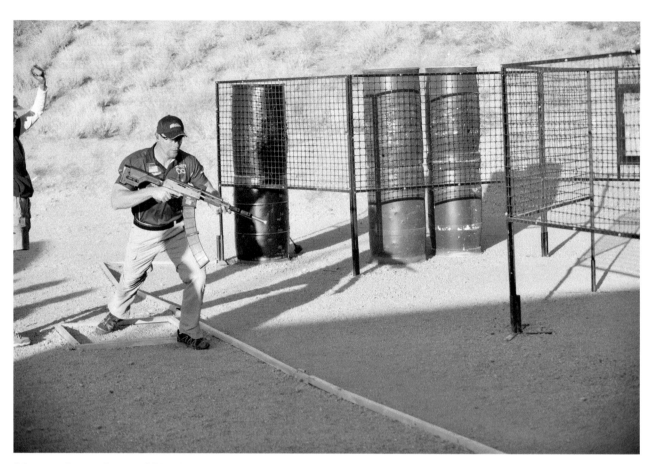

(above and opposite page) Match directors sometimes designate specific shooting boxes or shooting area, with fault lines, where shots must be fired to avoid penalty.

The International Defensive Pistol Association (IDPA) is an offshoot of IPSC-style shooting, formed by shooters unsatisfied with the "gamesmanship" perceived to be prevalent within USPSA matches and rules. IDPA currently claims more than 19,000 members, and its competitions differ from IPSC's primarily in their rules structure, which establish competitions leaning more towards self-defense or tactical-style shooting, rather than a test of pure shooting skills, as some view the matches of IPSC. Both USPSA/IPSC and IDPA have been extremely successful in the U.S., but primarily as organizations that promote and sanction pistol competition. 3-gun, while influenced by USPSA rules already in place, has developed outside the vacuum of any one governing

body, although 3-Gun Nation is quickly becoming the entity that bridges many matches and clubs together.

A 3-Gun event, or match, is a collection of individual courses of fire, commonly called "stages." During each stage of multiple targets, a competitor, under the direction of a range officer, negotiates that stage— keep in mind that this is an action sport, so there's lots of moving around from place to place, from one bank of targets to another, and so on—engaging each target as described during the stage briefing given by the range officer before the timer buzzer goes off. That briefing varies in its instructions, ranging from strictly regimented courses that must be shot in a specific sequence, to free-form design, where the competitor is free to map their own strat-

After a stage description read by the range officer, competitors are often given a quick five-minute walk through period to look at the stage.

egy. A stage can have a specific starting area as limited as a small "starting box," outlined by wood or metal staked into the ground. Stages can also have specific shooting areas, where certain targets must be engaged using particular firearms. Fault lines are sometimes present, and they mark the end of an area of movement for a competitor—no shots may be fired outside of a shooting area or forward of a fault line without receiving penalty, which is applied to a shooter's score in extra time.

After the stage briefing, the squad—a designated number of competitors that rotate through the match shooting each of the stages as a unit—is allowed a walk-through period. Often limited to five minutes, competitors get a chance to see

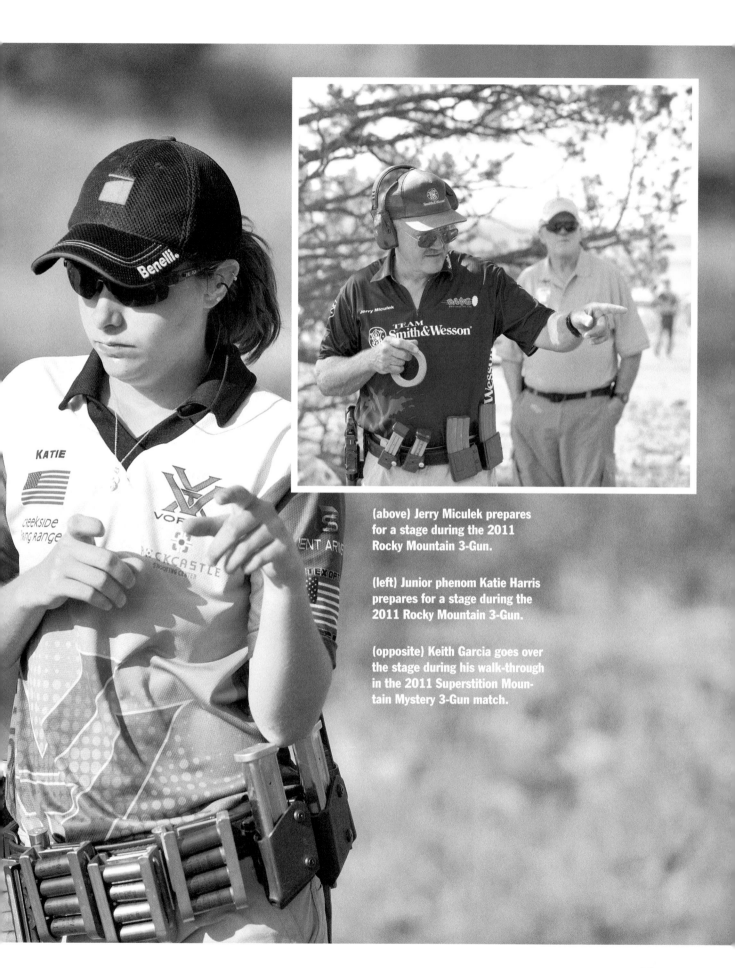

(above) Jerry Miculek prepares for a stage during the 2011 Rocky Mountain 3-Gun.

(left) Junior phenom Katie Harris prepares for a stage during the 2011 Rocky Mountain 3-Gun.

(opposite) Keith Garcia goes over the stage during his walk-through in the 2011 Superstition Mountain Mystery 3-Gun match.

each target, walk the stage as they anticipate they'll run it when it's their time to shoot—this might include planning out where best to reload, how to approach and shoot over, under, or around a barricade, etc.—and ask any questions of the range officer.

It's here that a 3-gun stage can get a bit complicated, and even confusing. At a given match, there are numerous types of targets one might encounter. There are multiple sizes and types of paper targets, with the IPSC-style cardboard torso/head target being the most common. (3-Gun Nation recently developed a new bull's-eye-type paper target that will likely become more common in local club matches.) Steel targets also show up in various forms, ranging from simple knock-over pieces of circular or rectangular steel sitting on top of a target stand, to advanced steel target systems manufactured by MGM Targets and others. Hinged steel "poppers," "plate racks" (six or more pieces of circular steel affixed to a target stand), static steel plates affixed to target stands, and reactive steel targets that move when struck are all used. Auto poppers are popular for rifle stages—here, the popper goes down when hit, then mechanically resets itself without anyone having to go downrange. Most reactive steel targets require a range officer to call "hits" when used in competition. Clay birds are another common target on some stages, and they're usually found in the form of a static target placed on a target stand. Clays are also thrown, just as they might be in

Match directors often use various forms of props and constructions to provide interesting target presentations.

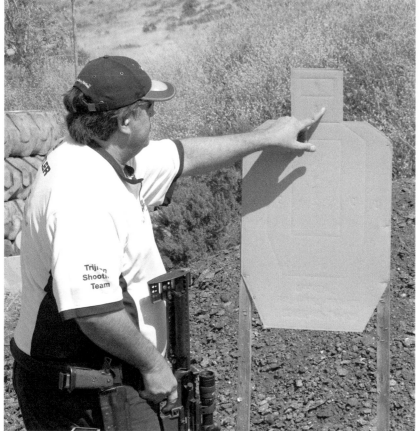

(above) Knock-over, static steel targets are common in 3-gun, such as this piece of steel placed during the 2010 Blue Ridge Mountain 3-Gun.

Taran Butler (left) points out scoring zones on a typical IPSC target used at many 3-gun matches.

traditional sporting clays, trap, or skeet clay bird games, adding a further degree of difficulty to 3-gun.

Moving targets offer yet another challenge. Often activated when a popper is knocked down, these limited-exposure targets come in many forms. Usually a paper target, the presentation can be moving from side-to-side, often only partially exposed. It can also turn towards the competitor, and then away again after a moment. There is also an "attack target" which accel-

erates toward the competitor before disappearing out of view. Limited-exposure targets can be *extremely* challenging!

Finally, there are the specialty targets—Texas Stars, Spinners, the Propeller Rack—that use gravity and balance to move in various directions. There are many specialty targets, especially the popular ones from MGM Targets, that provide fun and challenging shooting in 3-gun.

Ultimately, depending upon the stage description given by the range officer, all these different types of targets and presentations can be presented for specific or multiple firearms within a given stage—that means 3-gun is a thinking man's game, as much as it is one of pure shooting fundamentals and skill.

As with most action shooting sports, 3-gun is one that is measured in time. When shooting a stage, the competitor, under the direction of the range officer, will "stage" any firearms (i.e., put them in various places throughout the stage for pickup and use when they get to that portion), and, finally, receive the command to "make ready," with a specific firearm. Then, holding a timer that tracks each audible shot, the range officer pushes the timer's button, a loud "beep" goes off, and competitors rip through stages as fast as their skills allow. At the end of the stage, the raw time it took the shooter to complete the stage is recorded, then any penalties for procedurals or targets missed are applied to form a final stage time, or score. Each stage time is added up, and, as it is with golf, where the fewest strokes win a match, the 3-gun competitor who finishes an event the quickest, penalties included, is the match winner.

Matches vary in size (both competitor number and venue), and form. Major Matches, such as Superstition Mountain Mystery 3-Gun, in Arizona, which I'll cover later in this book, feature 250 or more shooters,

Like most action-shooting disciplines, 3-gun is one in which stages are measured in time—fastest to neutralize all targets is the winner.

(left) Static clay targets are sometimes placed behind falling steel poppers, forcing competitors to slow down during an otherwise extremely fast target array.

(above) Moving paper targets are common in 3-gun, including groups of them activated by a falling popper such as this bank of evil movers put out at the Tarheel 3-Gun match in North Carolina.

(right) It takes only one BB punching through to consider a clay target "broken."

(below) Most 3-gun stages are combinations of various types of paper and steel targets.

utilize a wide array of props and targets, and boast some of the fastest, wide-open types of stages in 3-gun. They often consist of short stages confined to three-wall bermed shooting bays, and the targets and scoring system combine to promote extremely fast shooting. The competition at Blue Ridge Mountain 3-gun, conversely, is a Major Match situated in the rolling hills of Kentucky, which provides a tremendously physically challenging natural terrain course of fire. The scoring and target placement penalize inaccuracy, especially with a rifle, so Blue Ridge becomes a very physical, accuracy-oriented test of skills.

At the local level, match stages are most often contained in shooting bays and limited to 100 yards, although some clubs certainly have the ability to hold long-range rifle stages. Fields of competitors can be anywhere between 20 and 100 in a one-day local club match, offering a wide range of shooting experiences.

No matter what the size or location of the shoot, scoring formulas, rule structures, target presentations, and match styles can vary wildly in the sport—there is, quite literally, a different face to 3-gun nearly everywhere you go. But, this is part of its core, and just one of the many reasons 3-gun is the most exciting discipline in all of shooting.

It takes a tremendous amount of guns and gear to shoot a major 3-gun match.

(left) Gravity moving targets such as a "Texas Star" or "Whirly Gig" will be seen at many matches.

(above) In 2012, 3-Gun Nation, in partnership with Birchwood Casey, developed a new 3GN Pro Series Target for 3-gun.

(below) White, IPSC-style targets are often designated "No Shoot," and competitors receive a penalty each time one is struck.

CHAPTER 2

WHY WE PLAY

The moment comes all at once. Desperately, you run it all through your head one final time—*Shoot four steel on the left, pivot right, load four shotshells moving to the barricade, take three in the first port, six in the left port. Dump shotgun, pick up rifle off table, remember to charge it, go to work … .*

From your periphery you see the last shooters return from setting steel, no more time to plan. You set your guns under direction from the range master, taking sight pictures, checking scopes, turning on red dots. You dry fire your pistol. Finally, there is only the inevitable. Nothing left but to step into the box, close your eyes, take a deep breath, and … .

The beep of the timer shatters the Zen-like world you have created, quiet reflection hammered away by the bass drum that is your pulse, the electric hum of adrenaline synthesizing through your head, racing past thought and carrying you into the moment. *Pop, pop, pop, pop … .*

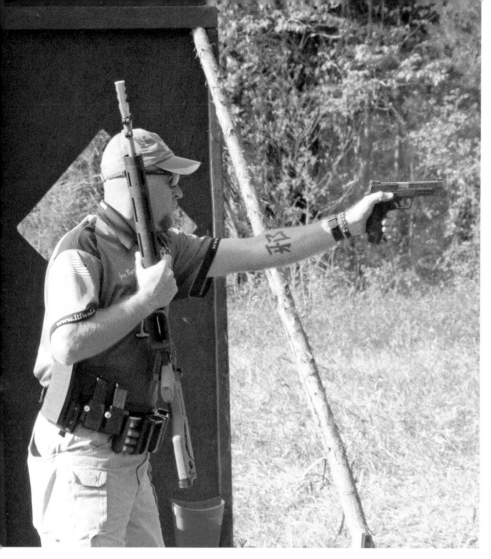

Not too long ago, most new 3-gunners were, in fact, veteran USPSA pistol shooters who had a fair amount of competition experience. That pistol experience translated into a working knowledge of the competitions themselves and provided a baseline of shooting skills that had been measured under the stress of the clock. Perhaps more importantly, at least for anyone wishing to excel, those shooters came to the sport of 3-gun with a fundamental experience in stage breakdown. In short, these pistol shooters needed only to add a shotgun and rifle to their shooting repertoires (which is plenty, to be sure), and they were off runnin' and gunnin' in 3-gun.

You are now only vaguely aware of the physical, your movements carried out by regimen, and you force yourself to focus on the bare minimum of self-instruction—*get your head down on the stock … front sight, front sight … breathe!*

Shotgun-rifle-pistol it goes, targets crashing in and out of view, sight pictures riding the wave of your heaving chest. "Hit!" bellows the range officer, nearly drowning out the perfect sound of a 55-grain bullet pounding a piece of steel more than four football fields away. It's orchestrated chaos, a crashing wave of excitement, panic, fear, and elation, all at once, all in that moment that belongs to you and you alone.

Welcome to 3-gun.

(above) The face of 3-gun is different at every match and venue, making 3-gun challenging—and never boring.

(right) The margins of error, and the difference between loss and victory, can be extremely small in 3-gun—which make it all the more rewarding.

I am not a champion 3-gunner, nor even an especially good one, in all honesty. I am a journalist by trade, one with unique access to the best shooters on the planet. But that access has had a profound effect on me over the last few years—as soon as I picked up a rifle and sent brass flying, I was immediately hooked on the sport. As 3-gun continues to grow, I am a typical example of the new shooters coming fresh into the game.

I, like a lot of new 3-gunners today, came into this game with very little competition experience and the critical knowledge base that comes with it. To us, 3-gun just flat out looked badass, and we had to give it a try.

You know what? That's all it takes. This game, if you give it any kind of a fair chance, has the ability to quickly morph into an obsession. In that basic way, it's like what golf becomes for the kids who outgrew their fascination with blowing up stuff. But golf is bland by comparison. Three-gun offers *so* much more. It's physical and grinding, and it has a hard edge to it, a 30-second all-out adrenaline dump that demands precision and

timing, while simultaneously requiring you give maximum physical and mental effort. To steal a phrase we use at 3 Gun Nation, "It's the X-Games of the shooting sports."

Unlike most sports, 3-gun is inclusive of the masses. You're not too old or too young, too rich or poor, and men, women, and junior shooters can all play. Even if you don't have any of the gear, chances are someone at the local club will loan you a gun, belt, holster, or shell caddy to get you through your first match. If you let them, many fellow competitors will help coach you, as well, pointing out a weak grip, how to load a shotgun faster, or something so specific such as

why one should move left three steps past the first barricade to most effectively engage an array of steel poppers.

So, 3-gun is an everyman's sport, but it also has an exclusive component to it. Point of fact, anyone can play. Too, at any size match, ranging from your local club to one of the biggest major 3-gun matches in the country, you may be squadded right alongside any number of the top 3-gun competitors in the game—and watching them burn down stages with remarkable speed, skill, and precision is likely to cause *your* engine to run in the red, which translates into a competitor pushing the speed beyond their skill set, resulting in an epic crash-and-burn stage performance. We all go through that—trust me—and, so, again, it's an inclusive sport. But 3-gun, at its highest levels, maintains an air of exclusivity, because the skills demonstrated in this arena—whether it be on sun-baked range bays or a pulse-thumping hillside over a natural terrain course of fire—must be *earned*. While there is almost certainly an elite few who exhibit a natural ability for picking up the game, the rest of us are left with one painful truth: competing with the best 3-gunners in the world takes a dedication unequaled in any other sport.

Still, anyone can have success in 3-gun. That success is, and should be, an ever fluid definition specific to the individual shooter. For me, success at my first match was defined by being safe, not breaking a rule that would get me disqualified, and, despite the inherent frustration from my demonstrated lack of skill and ability compared to others on my squad, having fun. For

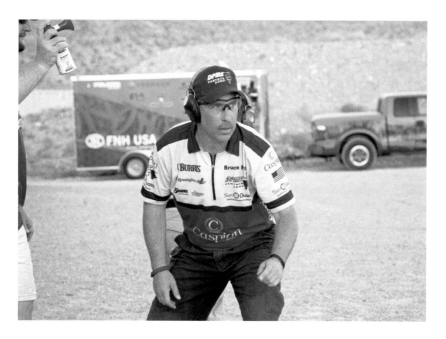

While 3-gun is certainly physical, the game is arguably best classified as a mental one, where focus is paramount.

most new 3-gunners, a safe, fun day on the range is the epitome of first-match success.

But, the more you play, the higher the performance ceiling that measures whether you're successful rises. Desired split times on target transitions decrease. Shotgun reloads must be conducted while moving instead of standing still. Or success can mean simply not to time-out on any stage in the match.

As with any sport, as performance improves and expectations begin to rise, so, too, at times, does the level of frustration. Like the golfer who hacks up the course for three hours, furious to the point he's ready to throw his bag of clubs in the lake, the 3-gun shooter will go to war on targets, miss reloads, and not have a clue where their rifle is hitting for nearly an entire match. Then, "it" happens. The shooter takes on that one bank of targets with a shotgun, or possibly even an entire stage,

and everything hits just perfect. Chest heaving, heart thumping, and out of breath, the command to "Unload and show clear" is given, the pistol re-holstered or shotgun returned to the rack and, with nothing more than a knowing look from the other members of the squad, the shooter knows he nailed it to the best of his ability. Better yet, he knows that everyone watching knows it, too. And, once you have that "it" moment, no matter how bad you had been that day or in other matches, you're completely hooked by 3-gun all over again.

"I think I'm addicted to 3-gun because of the challenge and the atmosphere of the matches," Team FNH USA's Dianna Liedorff told me. "There are so many components to the game that it seems like there is always room for improvement—unless you're Daniel (Horner) or Taran (Butler)! There is a great camaraderie with 3-gun shooters, and the natural terrain matches are so unique and beautiful!

"It's also pretty tough!" Liedorff continued. "The days are long and physically challeng-

ing. The weather doesn't always cooperate. With the added bonus from 3-Gun Nation of having money on the line, everyone is stepping up their game, and more shooters are coming to the sport to compete for titles and money!"

As the most challenging of any discipline within the genre of practical shooting, the face of 3-gun changes with every single match. Where one match is wide-open and extremely fast, the next is accuracy driven and painfully technical. Where prop-strewn stages are compacted into square bays at one venue, the next challenge forces competitors to run, jump, and climb over formidable, brutally taxing, natural terrain courses.

"The challenge of being proficient with three guns instead of one is what drew me in," said Colt's Clint Upchurch. "For me, it's kind of like starting over and getting to learn how to shoot all over again. Being presented with the many challenges that 3-gun presents and the great people associated with the sport are what makes it so appealing."

"I enjoy the additional challenge of three different platforms," said Samson Manufacturing's Bryan Ray. "There are many similar skills across rifle, shotgun, and pistol, but the types of targets we engage are obviously very different between the three. A shooter who is lightning quick with a handgun may not be able to shoot a long-range rifle stage very well—and shotgun is its own monster. The competitions are another draw to 3-gun. I don't think a more friendly or helpful group of people can be found within the shooting sports."

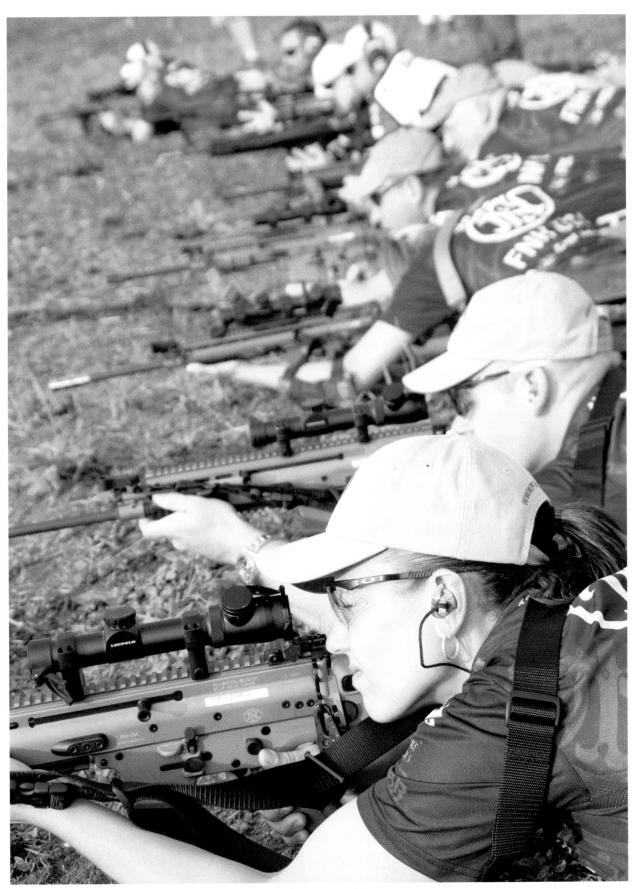

While you compete as an individual, teams do exist in the sport, and camaraderie is everywhere and at every level of 3-gun.

HIS

THE STORY BEHIND THE SPORT

I t's unfathomable to imagine where we might be today, in terms of the practical shooting sports, if it weren't for Jeff Cooper and the famous "Leather Slaps," at Big Bear, California. It was there that Cooper was joined by a group of like-minded individuals who'd come together and forever changed pistol craft as we know it.

Cooper, Weaver, Chapman—names that loom in lore over the entire firearms industry—are revered for the sum of their parts. Theirs is a doctrine for combat pistol shooting—the Weaver Grip and Stance, the Southwest Pistol League, Gunsite, the Modern Technique, modern competitive action shooting—all of it traces its roots or influence to Big Bear. Then, in 1976, Cooper and others formed the International Practical Shooters Confederation—IPSC—and the world finally had an organized body dedicated to the promotion of action pistol competition. But, as IPSC, and later USPSA (United States Practical Shooters Association), grew here in America, it wasn't long before a movement within the realm of action shooting began to take shape.

Soldier of Fortune—The Original 3-Gun Match

As action pistol matches gained in popularity, generally informal side matches for shotguns, and even the occasional rifle, began to pop up at local clubs. But it wasn't until a renegade magazine decided to sponsor a tactical-style shooting match that modern 3-gun was born. As such, the *Soldier of Fortune* World Championship 3-Gun Tactical Match is considered the father of all 3-gun competition.

"A milestone event took place in central Missouri, on 26, 27 and 28 September at the Ray Chapman Range in Columbia: The first annual Soldier of Fortune shooting match tested the skill of nearly 100 top-ranked competitors in combat pistol, *fighting shotgun and battle rifle events,"* wrote combat shooting luminary Ken Hackathorn, in the February 1981 issue of *Soldier of Fortune* magazine. *"The match was held in conjunction with the magazine's first annual convention."*

The association with *Soldier of Fortune* magazine set this match apart from the onset. As such, a highly skilled group of law enforcement and military professionals, as well as top-flight civilian competitors, converged on Missouri, for what would be a ground-breaking event in the history of practical shooting.

"The first SOF match was held in September 1980, in Columbia, Missouri," said veteran 3-gunner Mark Passamaneck. "One hundred shooters tested their mettle in an invitation-only match that had a match fee of $25. The terms 'soldier,' 'mercenary,' and 'adventurer' were associated with the competitors, both from a perspective of profession and personality."

"The crew of that first SOF event viewed it first and foremost as an law enforcement training event, and participating officers received a certificate of completion towards training credits if their departments accepted this type of training," explained John Gangl, another veteran 3-gun competitor and owner of JP Rifles. "However, civilians were more than welcome to compete, provided that they could furnish some credentials as to their previous experience in practical shooting, to serve as an indication that they could be expected to understand the basic safety requirements of such an event."

"Casual observers might suggest that such shooting events should be normal for U.S. military and police organizations," Hackathorn continued in his 1981 SOF article. *"Sadly, most training systems have less variety in their practical tests of skill than did this match, but Robert K. Brown and the SOF staff provided a proving ground for practical weapon-craft. Competitors in the invitation-only match were selected for their background and shooting ability. A very high percentage of them came from police or military organizations. The three match weapons were chosen on the basis of their importance in a combat role."*

The inaugural SOF match ran much differently than a major 3-gun match does today. Instead of stages of fire integrated with the use of multiple firearms on each stage (or even all three), the first SOF match really ran each firearm platform as a distinct, separate match, and each with its own champion. The scores were then tallied to formulate an aggregate champion and overall SOF winner.

"There was just one division at the start, and the gear of the top shooters included a .308 rifle, either an H&K 91 or an M1A, a single-stack semi-auto .45 pistol from various makers, and, interestingly enough, the Model 1100 Remington 12-gauge shotgun, which the entire top 10 of the inaugural match all shot," Passamaneck said. "Rifle scores were really what separated the top competitors from the pack."

The first match actually banned the use of rifles chambered in .223 Remington, a far cry from today's events, where AR-15-sytle rifles rule the day. In 1980, H&K 91 and M1A rifles dominated the field and comprised the gun of choice for the entire top 10. FN FALs and M1 Garands were in abundance, as well.

"First, and most critical, was the battle rifle match," Hackathorn wrote. *"Rifle-course ranges extended from 70 to 245 yards. The course consisted of 15 silhouette targets and six steel, falling plates. Time limit was a par time of three minutes. A competitor's score was upped by one point for each second he completed the course under the three-minute par time limit, and one point was deducted for each second over the three-minute-par time. Speed became an important factor. The rifle course had a score value of 360 points at par time. Thus, a rifleman capable of accuracy, fast shooting and quick movement, could increase his score well above the 360-point level.*

"Nine of the competitors managed to score above the 360-par level," Hackathorn continued. *"On the other hand, many shooters were humbled by this course. Most, however, felt— before the event—that target distances were not overly difficult and the shooting would be easy. Faced with the time-limit stress, two 40-yard sprints and having to reload, many shooters discovered that targets became elusive."*

Like much of the early IPSC shooting, Colt 1911s dominated the pistol class at the inaugural SOF. With a high number of law enforcement professional competing, service revolvers chambered in .38 Special were also in use. The course of

fire was one familiar to IPSC shooters of the day.

"They designed a simple course that required a total of 36 rounds," wrote Hackathorn. *"First, a total of 12 rounds were fired from the 25-yard line in two stages, a distance that duplicates the extreme long range normally encountered in combat.*

"Next, a series of drills were fired at the 10 yard line," Hackathorn continued. *"After a total of 18 rounds from this distance, six more rounds were fired from the seven-yard line."*

In the shotgun match, the Remington 1100 was the dominant choice by the top competitors, but, with many military and law enforcement professionals in the mix, there were various pump shotguns on the firing line, as well.

The shotgun match course of fire provided what was certainly one of the earliest practical shooting uses of steel targets for a shotgun stage in the U.S. In it, frangible clay birds were affixed to the center of 18x24-inch steel plates. In the first phase, competitors were armed with shotguns loaded with five rounds of buckshot and were required to break each clay bird from a distance of 25 yards. The drill was repeated at the 15-yard line, with a par time of 4.5 seconds.

In the second phase, competitors fired rifled slugs at silhouette targets, five shots from 25 yards, then a reload and a run forward to a place of "cover," where they fired at three additional targets. While the round count is low by today's major match standards, the use of movement, multiple firing positions and, most importantly,

mixed loads within a single stage (in this case, buckshot and slugs), are hallmarks at many major matches today.

"In both phases, match accuracy was important, and shooting technique really counted," wrote Hackathorn. *"Few people in the U.S. understand the technique of the fighting shotgun. Although the riot gun has a macho image, few users can achieve maximum performance with it. We all have heard gunshop-commando comments about just pointing the riot gun in the general direction, pulling the trigger—and everything will go down. In the SOF practical shotgun match, the big boys knew better. They shot from the shoulder, used a flash-sight picture and achieved well centered hits. All top 10 finishers used Remington 1100 shotguns."*

The inaugural SOF match was won by Raul Walters, a top IPSC pistol competitor and local businessman who went on to found one of the most successful real estate companies in the country (Walters' business success was largely due to the company's financing and real estate deals for a then-fledgling merchant—Wal-Mart). Walters won both the rifle and pistol competitions en route to a four-point overall victory. John Shaw, William Rogers, Charles Byers, and Bill Wilson—top shelf IPSC shooters all—rounded out the top five.

"Looking over the competitor list, one will see names such as Shaw, Enos, Leatham, Hackathorn, Heinie, Wilson, Plaxco, Cirillo, Fowler, and many others associated with firearms 'royalty,'" Passamaneck said. "Many of the founders of IPSC were also some of the pioneers of 3-gun. A large number of the now-famous names in pistol shooting tried their hands at the SOF matches in the early years.

Ironically, it's commonly held today that much of what led to the advent of 3-gun was the result of some within the practical shooting community attempting to make a break away from IPSC. While not completely *un*true, the match clearly set out to establish an arena that would prepare professional and civilians to better handle firearms in practical application. What few realize, and what I didn't fully understand until being pointed to the *SOF* article, is that IPSC was there in the beginning. From the names of top competitors to the IPSC-style pistol match to Ray Chapman himself running and officiating the event, the founding fathers of practical shooting, of IPSC, has their stamps all over the birth of 3-gun. In fact, an advertisement within the 1981 issue of *SOF* claimed all three matches to be "IPSC-sanctioned," and that the assault rifle match would crown the "First IPSC National Practical Rifle" champion.

Yet, somewhere along the way, a divide emerged between the renegade match and the sanctioning body of practical shooting. For *SOF*'s part, there was advertisement rumored to be featuring porn stars, stories regarding alcohol, and a series of very public trials over contract killings by mercenaries reportedly hired from the classified pages of *Soldier of Fortune*. Around that same time, USPSA was formed as the American region of IPSC, which possibly severed some

connections between the people involved. Whatever the reason, the SOF match, while maintaining the top competitors, lost its association with IPSC/USPSA—and, in turn, and in a very real way, IPSC/USPSA lost much of the sport of 3-gun. While I don't know and can't report the full story of the disconnection, the fact is best illustrated by the reality that USPSA didn't hold its first Multi-Gun Nationals until well over a decade had passed after SOF had ushered in a new era in practical shooting.

"Overall, the SOF three-gun shooting event proved a great success," concluded Hackathorn. *"Thanks must go to Ray Chap-* *man and his staff, who provided a superbly run event and top-quality judges and range officers. Such skill is rarely seen in major events. Chapman and his staff have plenty of expertise, thanks to their participation in other shooting events such as the Bianchi Cup."*

With the birth of the SOF event, the sport of 3-gun was off and running—a wild and woolly affair to some, for others, a liberating break from the oppressive structure IPSC-style pistol matches were perceived to have. But, for all, the SOF match represented a new and exciting brand of shooting sports unlike anything any of them had ever seen before.

"The matches, fees, stage complexity, and equipment multiplied considerably after those first few years," Passamaneck said. "As the SOF matches continued on for just over two decades, other groups decided they could depart from SOF and offer a different style of match. The main differences were in divisions and stage design. Courses started to become faster, favoring higher capacity rifles such as the AR-15."

"Three-Gun as been around since the early '80s," said veteran competitor Bruce Piatt. "At the time, the Soldier of Fortune World 3-Gun Tactical Championship was the richest event of the year. Remember,

in the early '80s, there were only four major matches to shoot—four, that's it. Steel Challenge, Bianchi Cup, IPSC (pre-USPSA) Nationals, and the Soldier of Fortune 3-Gun. The SOF match was an 'all-surprise stage,' buckshot and slug, long-range rifle, full-power, iron sighted pistol—a true combat match. The match had the highest prize structure of the time: $10,000 to the winner of the top 16 man-on-man shoot-off, not to mention the prizes for the match itself. For many years, the number of 3-gun matches were limited to SOF, USPSA 3-Gun Nationals, and the Miller Invitational 3-Gun Match—yes, Miller Beer sponsored this match in Fulton, New York, every year."

For many top shooters, SOF was an eye-opening experience. Sure, they were accustomed to high-level matches, but mostly ones that relied on known courses of fire, strict range rules, wide-open race equipment, and square shooting bay design. For even the top practical shooters in the country, their first experience in 3-gun proved to be something radically different.

"Nineteen ninety-seven was my first year there," said Tony Holmes. "The first year there was a big learning curve for me. It was basically an all-Tactical match. Scored major/minor with pistol and rifle, all buckshot and 12-gauge only, with a couple of slugs thrown in. Rifles could be shot with only certain battle-approved optics per SOF's guidelines.

Veteran competitor Tony Holmes has shot 3-gun for many years and was a winner of the famed Soldier of Fortune Match.

"All scoring with rifles was done by optic or iron sights. Each was given 100 points for the highest score posted per stage, and each stage was scored differently. You actually had to read the stage description for each stage and decide how you would attack it—with either speed or points—and points almost always won out. This type of match was different than others, because most of the other 3-gun matches I had been to and seen were being shot with Open guns. Everyone at SOF shot basically Tactical, and rifle was 50/50 as to sights, when I started. In the early years, all guns were iron sights. They started allowing bipods on rifles around 1999."

The SOF match had its own distinct flavor, a characteristic that remains prevalent in the sport of 3-gun today, as each match director and crew put their unique stamp on the game at any given match. But, while that individualism in match design and philosophy flourishes today, it all started with SOF.

"Some felt that the World Championship 3-Gun (WC3G) venue was rather harsh and unaccommodating and may have had somewhat of a boot camp culture to it," said JP Gangl, founder of JP Rifles. "Granted, some of the staff members were a bit over the edge, but all that added to the ambiance. Actually, there is much to be said about a competition in which gamesmanship was frowned upon and complaining or protesting was highly discouraged. Did that make it less fair for shooters? I would submit that, over the long run, it was more than fair, and certainly more expeditious, with the nearly complete lack of whining, nit-picking, re-shoots and protesting that's tolerated in other venues.

"The expectation that a shooter will not be allowed to subvert the stage intent due to some weakness in targets, props, or stage layout allows for more creativity in stage design," Gangl continued. "As it so happens, multi-gun culture, as it exists today, has benefited greatly from the World Championship 3-Gun mind-set. Multi-gun shooters (for the most part) are willing to shoot under a broad range of circumstances—weather, rule sets, and shooting requirements—asking only that equipment classifications are known in advance and somewhat consistent from event to event."

This singular approach to match presentation, not to mention the fact that competi-

tors finally had a venue where they could shoot all three guns in a "practical" competition, immediately elevated the Soldier of Fortune match to among the most revered shooting competitions of its day. While certainly still held on the periphery of the shooting sports, 3-gun had a signature event in the SOF match.

"The WC3G was really analogous to the NRA Bianchi Cup, regarding its stature as an event, complete with semi-formal banquet, a real awards ceremony, and a cash purse," Gangl said. "If it had a problem, that may have been its association with the *Soldier of Fortune* magazine, the perception of which was not accepted in much of the law enforcement community. When the event and the magazine parted company, and the match's name changed to

the World Championship 3-Gun Tactical Match, many more law enforcement agencies accepted the match as an accredited training event for their officers."

Beyond the sometimes over-the-top range staff, the association with a renegade magazine that catered to the world of mercenaries, the awards, and even the cash purse, the attraction for most shooters in the early days of the SOF match was the shooting itself.

"Other concepts that worked very well for the event were the five-man squad format and semi-surprise or full-surprise stage system," Gangl said. "The five-man squad allowed for the four-man team event (with

Bruce Piatt, a five-time winner of the Soldier of Fortune 3-Gun, readies for a stage.

SOF Patch – Though it has been gone for many years, the SOF match lives on today in several major Outlaw 3-gun majors across the country.

a fifth-man spare) and made possible stages on which all five shooters were on the line shooting at once. Again, this resulted in some truly creative stages."

Surprise stages and manageable squad sizes set the stage at SOF for many competitors, and innovative events such as team-on-team shoot-offs set the match apart from most other shooting competitions.

"Although you did not have to participate in the team event and could register as a solo shooter, many teams did compete, and the five-man squad allowed them to stay together during the entire match and be slotted together for the team shoot-off elimination stage, a great concept in itself. There is no doubt that the team stage and team-on-team shoot-off were the highlights of this event and a great spectator draw."

Billed as a Tactical event, SOF's surprise-stage concept appealed to the growing number of shooters who felt the practical side of practical shooting was

being increasingly replaced by a more purely competition/sport philosophy. With no chance to walk through stages beforehand, SOF became distinctive.

"The semi- or full-surprise stage expectation prevented the 'choreographing' of the stage by shooters and required participants to remain somewhat fluid in their stage prep, rather than locking into some hard plan," Gangl explained. "This adds to the excitement and asks the real-world question, can the shooter think on their feet and improvise? Let us not forget that the common denominator among practical shooters is the addiction to the adrenaline rush."

More than anything, shooters who remember the old days of the SOF match continually refer to the stage design. Scoring rules implemented at the stage level for each specific stage, instead of across the board and for the entire match, enabled match designers to come up with stages unlike most shooters had ever seen before.

"Stage design and target designs were some of the most creative I've ever seen," Gangl said. "The scoring system was the foundation for the current Multi-Gun Association rules, with one fundamental difference. Where the multi-gun format today has become lock-stepped into a scoring system, due to the use of a program that accepts only predetermined values, the WC3G scoring system allowed for greater flexibility, with each range officer responsible for the design and proofing of their stage and free to use any type of scoring system as long as it made sense and was applied fairly to all. This may have been a basic time-only scoring system (based on raw time plus penalties in seconds), but, in some cases, it was a points system within some type of time restraint. The basic philosophy was to ask questions about real-world performance based not just on all-out speed, but on one's ability to manage their energy wisely and avoid mistakes under pressure. Whatever the raw stage results, the stage was converted to match points for the final aggregate."

USPSA Multi-Gun Nationals

By the late 1980s, the success and popularity of SOF had elicited an ironic effect. If one subscribes to the notion that SOF was founded, at least in part, as a tactical alternative to the "game" IPSC-style shooting had become, then the debut of USPSA Multi-Gun raised some eyebrows. From the onset, IPSC was formed as much to further combat pistol *doctrine*, as it was to establish the competitive arena in which to test and compare the competitors. But, as games so often do, the competition format itself, at least to some, had become more about pure competition and less about the practical side of the sport.

The popularity of the SOF match, to some degree, is no doubt owed to the "Tactical" style in which the competition was presented—physical and demanding, with full-surprise stages and combat-approved gear. However, if that been the only appeal of 3-gun, then the sport might have stagnated with just the SOF match alone. Instead, as this radical shooting sport gained popularity, a new form emerged under the auspices of the USPSA.

"In the early '90s, another multi-gun venue appeared out of the USPSA handgun format," Gangl said. "A small number of practical pistol shooters, with the influence of some who had shot in the existing SOF matches, decided to hold another national-level event under the USPSA rule set but modified to work with three guns. With the SOF match filling up by January or February of every year, there was a demand for another multi-gun match to accommodate the increasing interest in this sport. The first two of these events were held in Long Island, New York, and, for obvious reasons, moved to a more hospitable location, the Clark Shootout Range, in Shreveport, Louisiana."

Unlike SOF, where competitors "fought" their way through blind stages and used multiple firearm platforms within a given stage, USPSA Nationals set a limit of one gun per stage; ultimately, multiple Nationals champions were crowned.

"Initially, in order to work with the existing USPSA-type scoring system, the three guns were not mixed in any stage. The stages were all firearm-specific," Gangl said. "Also, there were no equipment classifications at the start, and most shooters shot in what would now be considered the 'Open' class, in which any gun configuration was allowed, as long as it was deemed safe.

"The first multi-gun match I attended personally was the second Long Island match," Gangl said. "I attended the 3-Gun Nationals every year after that. However, with my first opportunity to attend the SOF match, I realized there was another perspective on multi-gun competition altogether, one that attracted a much larger number of shooters who had a completely different take on the equipment and stage design. It was obvious that this was a more dynamic and pragmatic application of the multi-gun discipline, one that seemed to attract a highly dedicated and competitive group of people from LE, military, and civilian populations.

"Eventually, USPSA adopted equipment classes similar to the SOF/WC3G format, to bring those shooters under its tent and encourage them to shoot the USPSA-style events," Gangl continued. "These equipment classifications have now become one of the fairly consistent threads between most of these events."

Superstition Mountain Mystery 3-Gun

While SOF remained the preeminent 3-gun match in the country, a new form of 3-gun

began in the Arizona desert. In 1996, Superstition Mountain Mystery 3-Gun (SMM3G) debuted and, to some shooters, became everything SOF wasn't—and should have been.

Wide open and smoking fast, SMM3G established a new 3-gun philosophy based mostly on square-bay stages littered with some of the most entertaining and creative "props" seen in shooting. Combined with the allowance of Open-class race equipment, SMM3G quickly established itself as a new and exciting brand of 3-gun.

"The match has grown from 67 shooters, in 1996, to 275 shooters, in 2010," said Dan Furbee, SMM3G match director and founder. "I saw a need for a quality match. Prior to 1996, the only real serious 3-gun competition in the U.S. was the Soldier of Fortune match, in Las Vegas. SOF wouldn't allow competitors to use IPSC-style race guns or any other high-tech innovative gear, other than military or SWAT-approved equipment. By opening the competition field up to open-class shooters, the 3-gun competition as we know it today burst forward."

Superstition has proven to be a seminal 3-gun match in the history of the sport. The innovative thinking in stage design and the use of props had a major influence on the sport's awareness spreading through the shooting world. And ,with stages seemingly catered toward the use of race guns, a new style of 3-gun was born at Superstition, as well. However, one could argue that its influence on rules and scoring is the largest lasting impact of the Superstition Mountain Mystery 3-Gun.

"With a further simplified scoring system designed to expedite stage reset time per shooter, in addition to the elimination of the power factor concept and recognition of the most common equipment classifications, the SMM3G celebrates its seventeenth year with the 2012 event," Gangl said.

"The International Multi-Gun Association (IMA) evolved out of the SMM3G event, the intent being to establish a standardized set of rules and equipment divisions for multi-gun competition," Gangl continued. "Presently, North American multi-gun competition is shot primarily under IMA rules or USPSA rules (with some exceptions). The IMA model has become the most successful and widely used at this time. The IPSC world body has also become involved in multi-gun competition in countries that al-

low the civilian ownership of the necessary equipment. However, while IPSC multi-gun is similar to USPSA, it only recognizes the Open and Limited divisions, with Limited requiring the use of iron sights only (i.e., no optics) on the rifle."

JP Rocky Mountain 3-Gun

By 2000, 3-gunners now had three established major national events in which they could shoot: SOF, USPSA Multi-Gun Nationals, and Superstition Mountain Mystery 3-Gun. The emergence of new matches proved the fledgling sport was finally experiencing growth. However, change was once again about to come to the world of 3-gun.

"In 2001, the SOF match split off from the *Soldier of Fortune* magazine and became the World Championship 3-Gun Tactical Match (WC3G)," Gangl said. "Colonel Robert Brown (Ret.), founder of the *SOF* magazine,

then decided to run the SOF match at the NRA Whittington Center. Consequently, in 2001, 2002, and 2003, the SOF match was held at the Whittington Center and the WC3G remained in the original Las Vegas location.

The split brought about a bit of confusion, nationally, over what exactly was what. In Nevada, you had the continuation of the match that had been SOF. Meanwhile, at the Whittington Center, a new match under the same SOF name emerged, one with much of the former crew and shooters in place.

"In 2002, Kurt and Eric Miller (et al) were awarded a contract to run the SOF match for the magazine at the Whittington Center" Gangl told me. "The *SOF* magazine then decided that it no longer wanted to

John Paul Gangl, founder of JP Rifles, was instrumental in the formation of the JP Rocky Mountain 3-Gun Match sponsored by JP Rifles.

be involved with the match, and JP Enterprises, Inc., stepped in as the major named sponsor, engaging the existing match crew to run the newly named JP Rocky Mountain 3-Gun Championship. This match is unique, as it is designed and held in the natural terrain of the Whittington Center, as opposed to the typically well-developed square ranges competitors were accustomed to. The added dimension of a natural terrain match cannot be underestimated."

By 2003, the WC3G was no more. The Rocky Mountain 3-Gun match had effectively supplanted both the WC3G and the SOF matches, developing its own unique brand of 3-gun over the years, as match directors changed. Today, JJ and Denise Johnson successfully run RM3G, and the match is very much a reflection of their idea of what 3-gun should be.

"As IPSC and, later, USPSA matured and changed, some of the rules and divisional designations spilled over into 3-gun," Passamaneck said. "In the late '90s, several matches that owed their success to SOF grew larger and more popular than the original, which had ceased to exist after the final match, in 2002. However, there were several 3-gun matches born in the 1990s, and Rocky Mountain 3-Gun followed on the heels of the SOF matches with some of the past officials and competitors stepping in and running the match 'Under New Management,' thanks in large part to its title sponsor of JP Rifles."

Ultimately, the legacy of the SOF match lives on today, in some form, at Rocky Mountain, and with that match's survival,

and the success of Superstition Mountain, the stage was set for 3-gun growth on a national stage. All the sport needed was a catalyst.

Randy Luth and the DPMS Tri-Gun

With Superstition, Rocky Mountain, and USPSA Nationals, among others, becoming established 3-gun "Majors," the sport of 3-gun began to build even more momentum, with new local and regional matches popping up at range facilities that had never before hosted a 3-gun match.

Then, in 2003, an innovative AR manufacturer, led by its self-made founder and owner, jumped into the sport full bore. In doing so, DPMS changed the sport forever. Here you had a match sponsored by a gun manufacturer, which in and of itself wasn't unique, but the way in which Randy Luth and DPMS approached hosting a match changed everything. I covered that first DPMS Tri-Gun Challenge as a staff writer and editor for the National Rifle Association (NRA), and I remember walking the prize table with Luth shortly before the conclusion of the match. We both sort of stared out across the row upon row of AR-15s, upper receivers, lower receivers, and a multitude of parts, almost all of it exclusively provided by DPMS that first year.

"What do you think?" Luth asked, not really looking at me or waiting for my answer. "Yeah, it needs a little more," he answered himself. What do you think we should put out?"

"Some Low Pros might be

cool," I answered, shrugging my shoulders in complete disbelief that anyone could possibly give anything more away.

Luth turned to a DPMS employee, asked for some number of Low Pros to be brought out, and the prize table grew ever deeper, just like that. I don't recall how many tens of thousands of dollars in product Luth gave away that inaugural Tri-Gun Challenge. And I'm not sure he ever knew the amount himself, because it didn't matter. Randy Luth had decided to set the bar.

At this point, DPMS had assembled what amounted to one of the first fully sponsored 3-gun teams in the sport. The company backed up that investment by putting on what became one of, if not *the*, signature 3-gun match of the season—and, after that first year, it wasn't merely DPMS product on the prize table. DPMS reached out to the entire industry for support, even direct competitors, and the result was arguably the deepest, most lucrative prize table in the sport.

"We first got involved in promoting competitive shooting, when Al Greco introduced DPMS to Jerry Miculek at the Second Chance shooting event, in 1998," Luth said. "Al suggested we sponsor Jerry and some other shooters, based on the fact that we had been donating many rifles to the Second Chance events over the previous few years. It was through Al that we made some deals with Jerry and Bruce Piatt. In the meantime, we began donating products to the few 3-gun events that were starting up in the late '90s and early 2000."

As DPMS grew as a company, Luth continually supported competitive shooting events around the country, as do many gun companies at varying levels. But few company owners and presidents actually get out and shoot alongside the competitors and customers. Luth, though, was never your ordinary gun company president, and, in a refreshing take on "knowing your customer base," Luth got bitten by the 3-gun bug.

"One event we donated to was the Wily Coyote 3-Gun event, in White Bird, Idaho, put on by Evolution USA (rifle makers Edd and Leanne Woslum)," Luth said. "It was at that event that I was physically introduced to my first 3-gun. The two dudes that got stuck with me were Bill Sahlberg and Pat Kelley, and they were the ones who got me hooked. I had no equipment other than my rifle—they set me up with a pistol, shotgun, and gear to shoot my first match. As you can imagine, I finished in last place, but, from then on, we saw an opportunity to promote our products in a new arena that would generate some "brass"-roots marketing for our rifles and accessories, similar to what we had done with grass-roots marketing at gun shows throughout the '90s.

As with any business, if the owner is active in the business at the customer level, then you automatically bring credibility to your product. It's sad to see so many firearms company owners who have no clue what's going on in their industry. My position was to get involved in 3-gun (and to use our products in the hunting arena, as well) to promote a new segment of rifle sales. If you want to

increase sales, then the best way is to go to a gun show and set up your table or booth and do one gun show a month for a year at different gun shows around the country—you will know *exactly* what's happening in the industry. Respect is earned by participation.

"We chose to sponsor 3-gun events to help promote our products in this new arena," Luth continued. "As a new competitor and owner, I felt that it was a great way to get shooters off the couch and involved in a fun and exciting venue, similar to what Dustin Emholtz had done with Zombie shoots at DPMS four years ago. Our industry has to adapt to the younger shooter, with new and exciting events and techniques for shooting guns. Our sponsorships to 3-gun was a win-win."

In short order, Team DPMS, with Jerry Miculek, Tony Holmes, Bruce Piatt, Dave Neth, Deb Cheek, and Randy Luth himself, became the top, if one of very few, full-fledged teams in the sport. With a top assembly of shooting talent competing at a high level that showcased the company's product in front of an emerging sport and customer base, Luth turned his attention to showcasing the sport east of the Mississippi.

"Our first Tri-Gun Challenge, in 2003, was a continuation of my interest in building new customers through the sport, plus, we had our own range to put on the event and a following of industry people we could tap into for sponsors, therefore we had a prize table that grew to over $200,000," Luth said. "It was great fun, as well as exposure for DPMS and our sponsors to help promote 3-gun."

For a lot people in and around the sport of 3-gun, it's hard to overemphasize the importance of DPMS' involvement in 3-gun. Never before had such a large gun manufacturer taken such an active role in the sport. The sponsored team featured many of the absolutely best shooters in the game, and the addition of the DPMS Tri-Gun match became a pivotal step in the sport's success.

The Tri-Gun brought major match access to roughly half the country, where before the sport had been mainly a Western phenomenon. Stages were fun and challenging, and the staff was top notch. Of course, the prize table became a lightning rod that sent shockwaves throughout the action-shooting community.

"People tell me that DPMS was a turning factor in 3-gun," Luth said. "I don't wish to take that credit, because there were so many people and matches nationwide that were as influential. However, we did put 100 percent of our efforts into sponsoring big and small matches across the country, putting the DPMS Shooting Team together in 2002 and beyond, with Jerry Miculek, Al Greco, Bruce Piatt, Tony Holmes, Deb Cheek, James Darst, Wayne Holloway, Kerry Dematos, part-timer Scott McGregor—all helped to bring awareness and credibility to the sport and to DPMS. All these factors helped to advance 3-gun."

"USPSA Nationals came after SOF in 1990, then SMM3G in 1997, RM3G in 2002," said Tony Holmes. "DPMS, in 2003, in its first year, had all of about 50 or more shooters that year. This is where I first met Randy

Luth and got his vision for what 3-gun/multi-gun should be and how the AR-15 had a place in it. Randy wanted and proved then that the DPMS Tri-Gun represented what all other 3-gun matches should be in regards to the quality of the staff and stages and the industry support for the game. He pushed and generated support for how the industry acts *today* in its support for 3-gun. If not for Randy Luth and DPMS Tri-Gun, along with Randy's persistence to make the industry stand up and take notice, I don't know if it would be where we are now."

Luth's impact on 3-gun goes beyond the obvious. Yes, his company made a great product

(top and left) DPMS and DPMS Tri-Gun Challenge founder Randy Luth eyes an aerial clay and prepares for a stage at the 2010 FNH USA Midwest 3-Gun Championship. (bottom) Luth takes on rifle targets during the inaugural Fallen Brethren 3-Gun match, in Texas, during the 2011 match year.

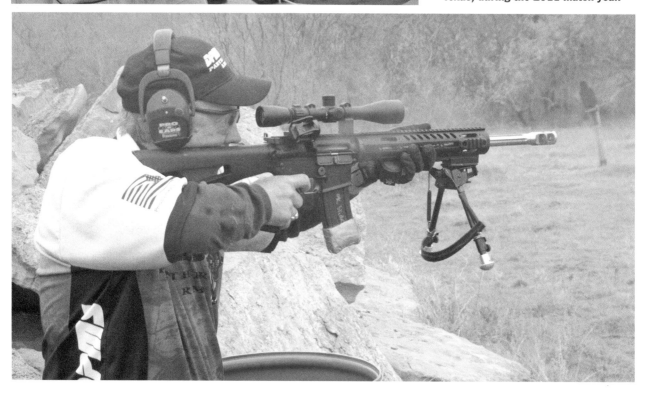

that was perfect for the sport, with options available to build a rifle essentially any way a customer desired. And, yes, Team DPMS went out and won match after match, so that Tri-Gun became the hottest ticket in the sport, with competitors from all over the country planning their work schedule, family vacations, and match calendars around the DPMS match. More than all this, though, it is the way in which Luth shared his position atop the sport that has had the most lasting impact. Instead of jealously guarding the enviable position his company had attained, Luth *pushed* rival gunmakers to get into the game right alongside him.

"Randy Luth has played a major part in promoting not only 3-gun, but shooting in general," said champion shooter Bruce Piatt. "Randy felt so strongly about the promotion of 3-gun that, even though he was the owner of DPMS, he called me, a sponsored DPMS shooter, and asked me to go to another AR manufacturer in an attempt to get another 3-gun match up and running—and now it looks like Ken Pfau, from FNH USA, has caught the same bug as Randy."

"I don't remember the details with Ken Pfau, but I am sure it was at one of the Shooting Industry Masters events that I encouraged him, as well as many other manufacturers, to get involved," Luth said. "Thank God they did. Tom Knapp and I also tried to convince Benelli to get involved in 3-gun four years ago or longer, and they resisted, but have finally seen the light. Our approach at DPMS was not isolationism or selfishness in order to protect our 'sandbox' in

3-gun, it was to get more manufacturers involved."

By 2007, the DPMS banner was flying higher than ever before. Now the second-largest manufacturer of AR-style rifles in the country, due primarily to the politically charged "black rifle revolution" that has swept the country, but also fueled by 3-gun sales, DPMS was acquired by Cerberus Capital Management, the same holding company that purchased Remington. Luth remained president of DPMS but, as with any sale of this sort, change was coming.

The most surprising change of all, at least for 3-gunners, came in 2010, in the form a disgruntled neighbor. After years of hosting signature matches of various shooting disciplines, a landowner adjacent to Randy's Del-Tone Luth Gun Club, home of the DPMS Tri-Gun, launched an all-out attack on shooting by challenging the Club's conditional use permit. Though to most it seemed a mere technicality,

FNH USA's Ken Pfau readies for a stage at the 2010 Blue Ridge Mountain 3-Gun match.

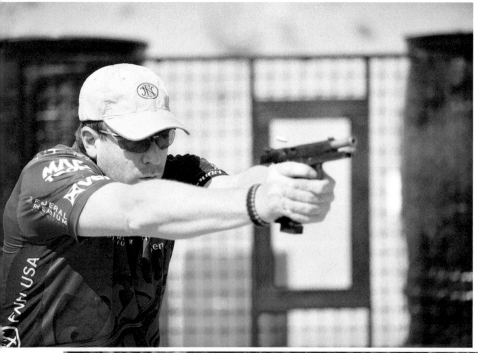

Team FNH USA's Ken Pfau takes on pistol targets during the 2011 Superstition Mountain Mystery 3-Gun (below) and during the 2011 ARF-COM-Rockcastle Pro-Am (bottom).

the challenge was upheld and the range was forced to cancel the Tri-Gun Challenge—a sad day for 3-gunners everywhere.

With Luth now retired from DPMS and the Tri-Gun match no longer in operation, one might think Randy's influence on 3-gun has ended. But that would be wrong, for the Luth ripple was just getting started.

FN Goes All-In

About the time DPMS was flourishing under Luth and the Tri-Gun was one of the major matches taking the sport to new heights, Ken Pfau set out to change the face of FNH USA—and he was going to do it in 3-gun.

Prior to Ken Pfau's influence, FNH USA had been many things to the firearms industry—but 3-gun wasn't really one of them. FN (Fabrique Nationale d'Herstal) itself was the legendary Belgian firearms manufacturer, steeped in history from John Moses Browning and his Auto-5 shotgun and Hi Power pistol to the legendary FAL full- and semi-auto rifles. More recently, the American arm of the company, FNH USA, had become a leading machine gun and rifle maker for the U.S. military. A student

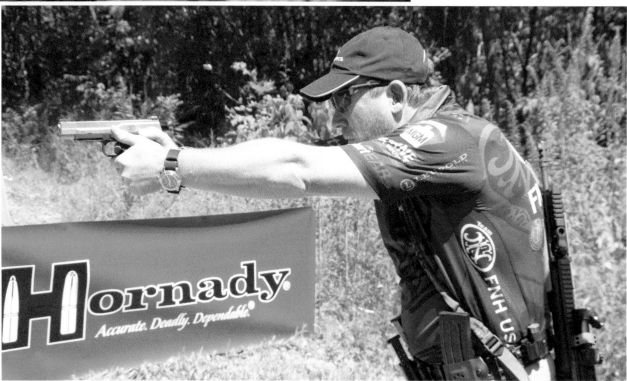

of fine sporting arms or hard military weaponry would more likely have FN on their short list of in-hand brands—but not a 3-gunner.

But, just a few short years ago, Pfau launched Team FNH USA to compete in 3-gun and serve as a team of ambassadors for the company, the product lines, and the sport. FN followed up the formation of an action-shooting team by becoming the title sponsor of a major 3-gun match—first the Midwest 3-Gun Championships, in Missouri, followed up by the formation of a completely new major 3-gun event, in 2011, with the debut of the FNH USA 3-Gun Championship, in Glengary, West Virginia. Like DPMS a decade before, Pfau and FN had gone "all-in" with 3-gun—and they'd gone one step further by sponsoring

a new TV show that sought to create a professional 3-gun tour—*3-Gun Nation*.

The 3-Gun Nation Effect

The sport of 3-gun was no doubt growing prior to the advent of *3-Gun Nation*. Matches such as the Fort Benning 3-Gun Challenge had pushed the sport in another new direction, as civilians leapt at the chance to compete in a match held aboard a military installation and get their hands on the "elite" firearms, vehicles, and gear normally used only by the U.S. armed forces.

Run by the U.S. Army Marksmanship Unit (AMU), the Fort Benning 3-Gun Challenge utilized the resources it had—soldiers—to staff and work an event in a way no other match could duplicate.

Stages were designed by AMU Action Team soldiers, and the competition was top notch. Finally, like the DPMS Tri-Gun, the prize table quickly became one of the deepest in the sport, attracting the top shooters in the game.

"After the demise of the WC3G event, in 2003," said Gangl, "a number of national-level multi-gun events have been organized and successfully run on an annual basis—the SMM3G, the JP Rocky Mountain 3-Gun, the DPMS Tri-Gun Challenge, the International Tactical Rifle Championship, in Gillette, Wyoming, the MGM Ironman event, in Idaho, the Fort Benning 3-Gun, and the

Deb Cheek runs her Open shotgun during the final Fort Benning 3-Gun Challenge in 2010.

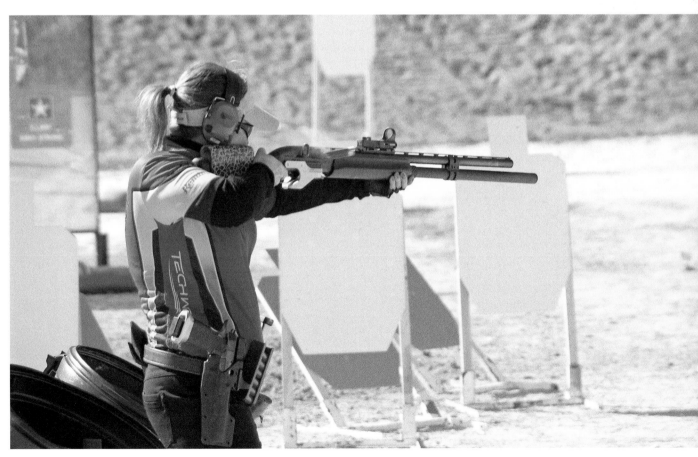

new Blue Ridge Mountain 3-Gun match—with more being added every year."

Meanwhile, a movement away from square-bay matches was beginning to take hold, with the landscapes of the Midwest, Blue Ridge Mountains, and the Ozarks attracting an entirely new type of 3-gun shooter, much in the way the Rocky Mountains so brilliantly backdrop the NRA Whittington Center. The Blue Ridge Mountain 3-Gun match provided only the second major match east of the Mississippi, and match director Andy Horner's often brutally demanding and physically challenging stage designs struck a chord among many shooters.

The MGM Ironman presented yet another face for 3-gun, with stages bordering on the ridiculous, as round counts doubled or tripled anything seen at previous matches—anywhere. Physical, arguably maniacal even, the Ironman gave 3-gun a match that only the truly dedicated—or the insane—could call home. As such, 3-gun had its radical, no-holds-barred, renegade event, complete with the adjectives that once were reserved for only one match, the Soldier of Fortune 3-Gun.

Then, in 2010, *3-Gun Nation* threw gasoline on the fire. At the onset, *3-Gun Nation* was seminal purely for the fact that it gave the sport a home; any successful sport has immediate and continuous access in the form of TV. With the television show and the continuous coverage on 3GunNation.com, the sport had finally found its headquarters.

"In the mid-2000s, things really started to heat up in terms of major matches," Passamaneck said. "While there were not a lot of local and regional matches, by 2010, there were at least a dozen matches that many would call major. That year also saw a new entity enter the 3-gun frenzy, *3-Gun Nation*. Some of the competitors didn't know what this new thing was, nor what it would do to the sport we loved. Suffice it to say, *3-Gun Nation* helped to bring the sport to the masses more so than any prior attempt."

3GN also put in place the groundwork for what will be fully realized in 2013—the 3-Gun Nation Pro Series, the first truly *professional* sport in action shooting. Much like BASS or FLW Outdoors in tournament fishing, the $150,000 3GN Tour established cash payouts for the top competitors, with the 3GN Championship becoming the sport's ultimate prize. Win the Championship, the title of 3GN Champion, and take home a cash purse of $50,000—previously unheard of in 3-gun.

But, beyond the money going to top shooters, the increase in sponsored shooters, the deeper prize tables at matches where 3GN cameras were rolling, beyond all that the 3GN name is beginning to contribute to the most important increase of all—participation. Since *3-Gun Nation* first aired, in 2010, there has been an undeniable spike in the popularity of the sport. From the addition of more major 3-gun matches (FNH USA 3-Gun and Fallen Brethren, both in 2011), to the amazing surge in 3-gun participation at the local match level, the contemporary face of 3-gun is changing. New shooters

are jumping into the game in record numbers. Where previously new shooters had come almost exclusively from the world of action pistol, today's new shooters are giving 3-gun a try after merely watching it on TV or YouTube.

Even more impressive? A fresh crop of top talent has infused the game with new vigor, as young, fit, athletic competitors are raising the bar on the national stage. And, with the advent of a professional 3-gun tour and the chance at never-before-seen cash and prizes, not to mention a noticeable

increase in corporate sponsorship of shooters, these new
3-gunners are talented, well
equipped, and hungry to make
their mark on the sport.

Multi-gun was surely enjoying some level of growth prior
to *3-Gun Nation*, yet 3GN has
become a major part of the equation behind the recent explosion
in its popularity. It is the latest
step in the colorful history that is
the sport of 3-gun.

"I've seen the shooting
industry jump in with both
feet and all of its support, and
I've seen the black rifle make

its case and prove itself as a
legitimate sporting rifle to the
general public," Tony Holmes
said. "I've seen and used the
new technology being introduced. I've seen the sport grow
each and every year, and I've
seen the birth of *3-Gun Nation*
to the world and how it has
brought 3-gun to TV.

"I wish I was 30 years old
again and knew what I know
now," Holmes laughed. "I'm
just glad to have been a part
of the explosion of 3-gun, past,
present, and now into the
future."

**Todd Jarrett runs a stage during the
final Fort Benning 3-Gun Challenge,
during the 2010 match year.**

THE JORS

Since the inception of 3-gun, in 1980, at the *Soldier of Fortune* match, the sport has rather evolved from the top down. Over the years, without any real system of local or regional matches to fuel demand, it was new *major* 3-gun matches that materialized across the country.

Some of these new major matches derived from the SOF match, while others sprouted in an attempt to offer something contrary to that very specific brand of shooting. In time, new matches were created, because it was becoming readily apparent that a real demand was building.

Today, 3-Gun Nation is building the foundation to meet that demand, with membership programs and club and amateur series points races that should help continue the increase in the sport at the grassroots levels—the very thing this sport has been missing. Meanwhile, at the top end, the 3GN Pro Series is taking the sport to a higher level than ever before—a professional sports league for 3-gun. But, even as the sport expands, it pays to remember that a big part of the soul of 3-gun will always remain in the Outlaw matches—the birthplace of the sport itself. Superstition, Rocky Mountain, Blue Ridge, Ironman—these matches were and are wide ranging in location, venue, and style, and all provide a distinct and unique face to the sport of 3-gun.

Superstition Mountain Mystery 3-Gun

The importance of Superstition on the landscape of 3-gun is arguably second only to SOF. While SOF established 3-gun as the renegade, anything-goes shooting sport on the periphery, Superstition brought real gun racing into vogue.

Held each year toward the end of March, Superstition has effectively ingrained itself in the sport as the unofficial kickoff to each new 3-gun season. Shooters from across the country converge on Arizona's Rio Salado Sportsman's Club, one of the finest action-shooting clubs in the country, some competitors dusting off gear that has been locked in gun safes for much of the winter off-season. The longest continuously running major 3-gun event in the country, SMM3G provides a fitting backdrop for the beginning of each new 3-gun season.

A large contingent of Open competitors drives in from the Western states, nearby in Arizona, or from as far as California, ready to put on a show at Superstition. Everyone loves the stage design at this match, but it's likely especially well suited for Open competitors, heavy on short courses and laid out wide (left) Famous for its use of props, this stage at the 2011 Superstition Mountain Mystery 3-gun required competitors to hold a putter at the start position.

(below) A competitor braces against a prop "Jeep" during the 2010 Superstition Mountain Mystery 3-Gun.

open for shooting. Competitors from every division, probably here more than anywhere, absolutely *rip* through these stages, shredding paper targets and steel with three, four, and five pieces of brass in the air at a time, as they send rounds downrange.

The shooting sports have a long history of using stage props across many disciplines, but nowhere is this more prevalent than in action shooting. Probably the most unique use of props comes from the world of 3-gun, and, within that realm, absolutely no one uses stage props quite like the crew at Superstition Mountain. Roller coasters, helicopters, harnesses, cars, walls—if you can climb over, under, around, or through it, Superstition is likely to find a way to incorporate it into a stage. The unique use of props is as much of a signature of Superstition, as is the wide open shooting so thoroughly enjoyed by most of its competitors.

The sport of 3-gun, largely due to the success and ingenuity of several matches that have evolved into what are now considered majors, is currently experiencing an unparalleled explosion in popularity, considered by most industry experts to be the fastest growing discipline in the entire shooting sports. With no match more pivotal than SMM3G, and with it being the first major of the year, Superstition has relied on innovation and out-of-the-box thinking to keep it a favorite for 15 years.

"SMM3G is known as the match to attend," SMM3G match director Dan Furbee said. "We use the natural terrain of the Arizona desert on some of our stages to enhance the shooting experience. Our stages utilize great props and equipment, along with innovative and fun targets. We were the first to use the LaRue self-setting rifle target

system. The SMM3G is also the first 3-gun match of the shooting season, and a lot of our dedicated shooters can't wait to get out of their snow-bound states to shoot in sunny Arizona. In addition to all that, sponsors such as DPMS, FNH USA, LaRue Tactical, Bushmaster, Patriot Ordnance Factory, JP Enterprises, Dillon Precision, Samson Manufacturing, Nordic Components, Trijicon, and SureFire, just to name a few, ensure fantastic prize tables that total more than $175,000 and make this the premier match of the shooting year."

Superstition also stands as a seminal match, due its overwhelming effect on the sport of 3-gun. Not only have stage design and target concepts been developed and proven in the Arizona desert, but rules and scoring doctrine that have influenced most of the major matches were developed by Furbee and his associates.

"SMM3G is the standard," Furbee said. "We developed the scoring system currently used in the 3-gun competition world. The International Multi-gun Association Rules (IMA) are accepted and used by most of the 3-gun competitions in the U.S."

Ultimately, the appeal of SMM3G derives from the fact that this is an event designed for shooters, by shooters. Understanding the wants and desires of the best pistol shooters in the country has evolved into a recipe that draws interest from shooters all over the country.

"All the serious 3-gun competitors are primarily competition pistol shooters who also happen to own these high-tech and very expensive rifles and shotguns," Furbee said. "We needed places and events where we could

Trapr Swonson takes on rifle targets through a "brick wall" barricade at Superstition Mountain Mystery 3-Gun.

compete with our other 'toys' and have a little fun. It's turned into a monster, and it's getting bigger! All any pistol shooter has to do is come to one of these matches and they'll be hooked."

Texas Multi-Gun Championship

Formally known as the Larue Tactical 3-Gun, match director Sheldon Carruth and his crew completely changed the face of this match and renamed it Texas Multi-Gun, in 2011. By all accounts the change was an emphatic home run.

Larue was retained as the major match sponsor, meaning there was no shortage of armadillo tactical bottle openers or barbecued pork from Larue's famous chuck wagon. More importantly, Larue provided an immense amount of support for the match itself, and the result was one that immediately elevated Texas Multi-Gun to become one of the premier events on the national Outlaw 3-gun circuit. Amazingly, nearly

400 competitors shot through the match—on time—during the 2011 Texas Multi-Gun.

"Match Director Sheldon Carruth and his team did a fine job with designing and running the match," wrote Bryce Towsley, in an article covering the event on 3GunNation.com. *"This is the first big 3-gun match on the relatively new Best of the West Shooting Range in Liberty Hill, Texas. The horseshoe-shaped range had all the stages close together for easy access, but each stage had plenty of room for a no-compromise design."*

The 2011 match had a World War II theme that, much in the tradition of Superstition Mountain, was nothing short of spectacular in the authenticity and creativity of stage props. Telephone poles were turned into palm trees, and trash dumpsters were transformed into Higgins Boat landing crafts. In short, the theme was carried out so thoroughly, the match had the unique backdrop of a World War II battle straight out of a John Wayne movie.

"While the match enjoyed excellent industry support, the main sponsor for the match was Larue Tactical," Towsley wrote. *"In a unique and much appreciated gesture, they also supplied lunch and all the drinks. The theme for the eleven-stage match was famous battles of WWII, but this event clearly was designed by 3-gun competitors who understand the game. The stages were fast and challenging and laid out for trigger pullers. I didn't see any mind-game stages, hidden targets or procedural traps, just well thought out stages that challenged even the best shooters. The R.O.'s were all friendly and competent."*

Competitors left Texas amazed by the use of props, impressed by the staff, and blown away by the stage design. Message board forums all over the Internet lit up, singing praise for the new face of the Texas Multi-Gun Championship.

"I am completely amazed at how well the match ran and at the quality of the stages and props," said Team FNH USA's Dianna Liedorff. "In the past, I've heard shooters shy away from new matches or a change in direction of a match the first year, in order to let them 'work the bugs out,' but that certainly didn't apply to this match. It seemed like they have been doing this for years. The ROs were very skilled; each had a job, and together they worked like well-oiled machines."

Midwest 3-Gun Championship

Steel, steel, and more steel has become one of the interesting themes of Ken Flood's Midwest 3-Gun Championship. Great stages, with ample use of reactive targets littered across rolling terrain have contributed to Midwest becoming a favorite

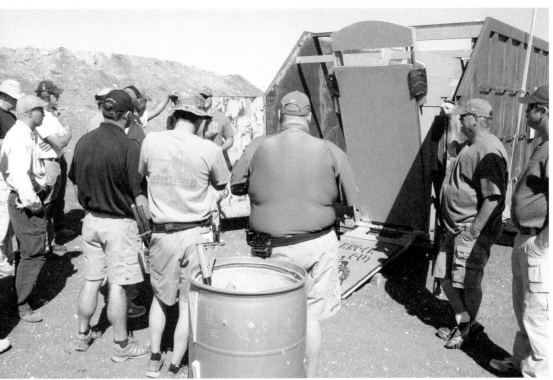

Taking a page from Superstition Mountain, the 2011 Texas Multi-Gun Championship used an amazing assortment of stage props—all themed in World War II battles.

Vintage-looking World War II military props at the 2011 Texas Multi-Gun Championship set the tone for what was one of the most talked about matches of the season.

on the national 3-gun circuit, with Midwest enjoying explosive growth since its debut seven years ago.

"We started the match at the request of Randy Luth, former owner of DPMS, to have a sister match with the same rules as the DPMS Tri-Gun Challenge," Flood told me, going into the 2011 match. "We started with about 120 shooters and expect 230-plus this year."

Step to the firing line at Midwest, and it's pretty clear what's bringing more shooters to Missouri each year. Piles of spent brass litter a course of fire that stands as a solid mix of target presentations, from long-range rifle over vast expanses of real estate to built-up square range designs that challenge the top shooters in the world.

"The match utilizes both improved-type traditional ranges, as well as natural terrain," Flood said. "We put emphasis on rifle accuracy in the form of partially concealed paper targets, as well as steel out to 400 yards. We also like to feature a high round-count shotgun stage of at least 34 rounds. The most defining quality, in addition to our excellent range officers, is the challenge of each stage and their creative design and effective management."

Midwest was one of the original matches on the 2010 3-Gun Nation Tour. Today, along with most major 3-gun matches, the match is a 3GN-Affiliated event, where 3GN Divisional, Semi-Pro, Amateur, Lady, and Junior points are on the line. The venue and challenge combine to make Midwest a favorite among shooters.

"Our match is a good fit, because it's one of the top 3-gun matches in the U.S. and we are centrally located," Flood said. "We'll also draw competitors who will be attending the NRA Bianchi Cup, which is the week after our match and 20 miles away. We expect many international competitors, as well as many of the top U.S. shooters. We want to be a part of the 3-Gun Nation, because it's going to be the most exciting thing to ever happen to 3-gun and will certainly propel the sport into the limelight of the shooting world."

MGM Ironman

From giant slides to zip lines to funky firing positions to round after round after round of ammunition, MGM's Ironman is a multi-gun competition unlike any other. Win it, and most veteran competitors will consider you one of the toughest 3-gunners around. To do so, you must fire well over 1,000 rounds of ammunition from every type of conceivable firing position. You will shoot at sniper distances until your eyes grow weary, rip through CQB-type stages at a break-neck pace, and pound away with shotgun slugs at extreme range until your shoulder aches. Do all of this without breaking you or your gear, and you just might just survive the MGM Ironman.

"We came up with the idea for the match, because we like to shoot a lot," said MGM Targets company president and match founder Mike Gibson. "We like all our guns, and we like to shoot all of them every chance we get. Traditional 3-gun before our match would be a format of three stages of pistol only, three stages of rifle only, and three stages of shotgun only."

Debuting more than a decade ago, the MGM Ironman forever blew the traditional concept of 3-gun matches out of the water. Today, the Ironman is a grueling three-day marathon in the Idaho desert, where competitors shoot all three guns on each and every one of the Ironman's 10 or more eight-minute stages. In a word, the Ironman is, quite simply, intense.

"Most stages at any 3-gun in the country are over in less than two minutes, some in less than 40 seconds," Gibson said. "We have an eight-minute par time on each stage—and they're fun and crazy stages. Just go and Google "MGM Ironman 3-Gun." Shooting from the back of a moving pickup, shooting 32 birds launched from a trap house,

The zip line has become a signature stage at Ironman adding some truly unbelievable exhilaration to this already action-packed sport.

shooting your pistol and shotgun while you're driving a golf cart, shooting your pistol while you're sliding down a 285-foot zip line, shooting your rifle from a 20-foot tower, shooting two match-furnished full-auto guns on a stage (in addition to the three guns you brought with you), shooting bonus shots at 700 yards, a surprise stage that includes a 200-yard run, shooting three pepper poppers in a row with a shotgun, each of which launches two clay birds 30 feet in the air (so you have six birds in the air all at once), shooting 75 to 100 slugs out to 100 yards. Everyone will shoot at least 1,000 rounds at this match—assuming they hit every target with the first shot."

Sound nuts? Well, don't feel bad, because even the most experienced and accomplished shooters in the world require a deep breath before jumping into the Ironman.

"A shooter asked Taran Butler (a veteran 3-gun competitor with several titles) if he was coming back the next year," Gibson said. "Taran's reply was 'Hell no! After that match you have to buy three new guns!'"

Even without Butler, you can expect many top-ranked shooters back at the Ironman, as well as numerous non-sponsored shooters that come back to Idaho each year for the most challenging course of fire in the shooting sports.

"Shooters either come back every year, or they never come back," Gibson said. "Of the 150 shooters that we'll have this year, probably 70 of them have shot this match a minimum of seven or eight times previously. There is no other shooting discipline that creates an adrenaline rush like 3-gun, and certainly not one that lasts for up to eight minutes non-stop."

A thrill for many recreational and high-level competitive shooters alike, the MGM Ironman is also turning some heads within the military community. Due to its unique setting, challenging courses of fire, and its unrelenting demand on both the human body and gear used to compete, some U.S. soldiers are finding correlations between the Ironman and actual combat and are using MGM's brutal 3-gun event as training prior to upcoming deployments.

"Last year, we had five sol-

Outdoor writer Bryce Towsley breeches a door during the 2011 MGM Ironman.

diers from the U.S. Army 5th Special Forces Group, from Fort Campbell, Kentucky, come out and compete," Gibson said. "The sergeant major is right now on his eleventh deployment. They said this match was some of the best training they had ever had. This year, 13 guys from the Oregon National Guard, who are being deployed this Fall, are coming to shoot, using this match as one more component of their training. I don't think any of the other matches in the country are perceived as providing any significant training value to the military or law enforcement communities."

If it's a good enough test for the U.S. military, you can bet the Ironman is a worthy test of anyone's shooting ability. But, what sets this match apart is MGM's wicked idea of what a competitor must endure just

Team FNH USA's Dave Neth, with all three guns, runs one of the mammoth stages at MGM's brutal Ironman, which included negotiating some interesting props during the 2011 MGM Ironman.

MGM Ironman is famous for its use of unique props—especially the Slide, where shooters take on long-range rifle targets.

Competitors must clear their rifle and point it downrange before sliding down, where they reload and engage rifle targets all over again.

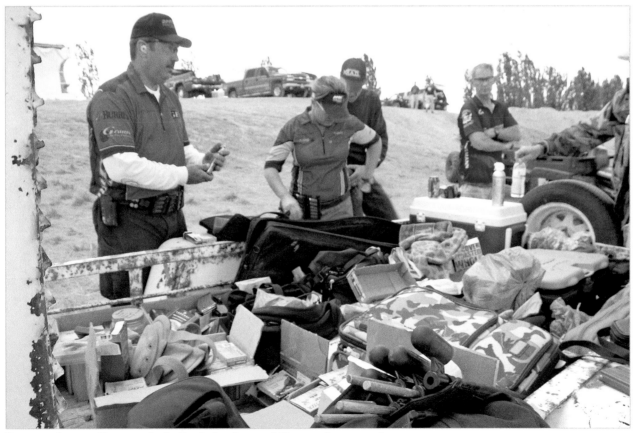

A group of competitors used a trailer to haul around the massive amount of equipment required to survive the MGM Ironman.

to take that shot, all 1,000 of them.

Northwest 3-Gun

Formerly run by R&R Racing's Robert Wright, the Northwest 3-Gun Championship was turned over to Scott Hawkins and Doug Hartley, in 2011, and, by all accounts, they have raised the bar even higher for the Pacific Northwest's largest major 3-gun match. And, while one stage can't make an entire match, it can sure put one over the top.

Such was the effect of the Crimson Trace Dark House stage, at the 2011 Northwest. With immense sponsor support, Northwest was able to provide a stage like no other for 3-gunners, much in the way the famous cave at Rockcastle is becoming that venue's signature.

"When Scott and I were planning this match," explained Hartley, "I decided to do a dark house, because I really like them and most people don't get to shoot in one very often. Iain Harrison, from Crimson Trace, got wind of it and asked if he could set something up. I told him sure—anything to get it off *my* plate! Next thing I know, he has this whole plan of night vision goggles and SBRs (short-barreled rifles) with infrared lasers—I was *stunned*. For the folks who got to shoot this stage, it was a once-in-a-lifetime opportunity to use some very expensive equipment."

Crimson's Harrison designed and built wall panels, brought them to the facility on a flatbed truck, and assembled the house. Meanwhile, Peter Lesbo of I2 Technologies & Systems Integration provided night vision goggles, while Next Generation Arms provided the rifles,

and Hornady kicked in 3,000 rounds of free ammunition. The combined efforts resulted in an uncommon 3-gun experience.

"It's pretty timely that we ran this stage not too long after our guys got Osama," Hartley said. "I don't know for sure, but I'm willing to bet that the same technology we used on this stage was used to ventilate our No. 1 Most Wanted guy. It's not fair to the guys on the receiving end, but, as my buddy Scott says, 'If you're in a fair fight, your tactics suck.' Incredible technology with devastating effect—so cool you don't know what to say afterwards except 'Can I do it again?'"

JP Rocky Mountain 3-Gun

An offshoot of what many consider to be the founding match of 3-gun, JP Rocky Mountain 3-Gun (RM3G) continues a proud legacy that began with *Soldier of Fortune*. But RM3G is important not only as one of the forefathers of the sport, but as a challenging course of fire that utilizes the rugged New Mexico landscape to create a completely unique event.

For nearly three decades, *Soldier of Fortune* magazine sponsored its SOF match, which was later named the World Championship 3 Gun Tactical Match (WC3G). That SOF match held a special spot as the original competition in 3-gun. Yet, despite its overwhelming popularity, match support eventually waned.

"*Soldier of Fortune* magazine decided it no longer wanted to be involved with the match, and JP Enterprises, Inc., stepped in as the major named sponsor and engaged the existing match crew to run what we called the JP Rocky Mountain 3-Gun Championship," said John Paul, president

of JP Enterprises. "This match is unique, as it is designed and held in the natural terrain of the NRA's Whittington Center, as opposed to the typically developed square ranges. The added dimen-

Rocky Mountain 3-Gun challenges competitors with natural terrain at elevation in the New Mexico Rockies, along with plenty of long-range rifle shooting.

sion of a natural terrain match cannot be underestimated.

"Each year, different people took care of different parts of the match, but now it's run by us," said match director Denise Johnson, who runs the event with her husband, J.J. "The stages have always been very challenging, with long-range rifle shots as a staple. It has developed into

a match with more multi-gun stages, longer bonus targets, and more moving targets for shotgun, and the match overall has been at the forefront of gun transitions that are safe and speedy."

Set at an elevation exceeding 6,000 feet, Raton, New Mexico's NRA Whittington Center provides a fitting backdrop for a physically demanding match. More importantly, with the tremendous space provided by NRA's signature range development, JP's Rocky Mountain

(above) Few shooting ranges enjoy the backdrop that is the home to the Rocky Mountain 3-Gun. Held aboard the NRA Whittington Center's 30,000 acres, Rocky Mountain offers stunning views.

(below) John Paul Gangl runs a rifle course during the Rocky Mountain 3-Gun.

3-Gun delivers rifle opportunities not common in competitive action shooting.

"The thing that makes it unique is the ability to shoot in

natural terrain and use rocks and hills as part of each stage's design," Johnson said. "Although the altitude gives people's hearts and lungs a workout, there is no other match where you can have a deer being chased by a cougar dash by the stage briefing, or have a brief shooting stoppage, while a bear looks at your targets and lets you know what he thinks of you."

While the setting is panoramic, to be sure, it's the diverse stages of fire, long-range rifle requirements, and the physically demanding nature of the event that drives competitors to come back year after year. As such, RM3G remains one of the most popular and well-respected 3-gun events in the country.

"JP RM3G is one of the premier events of 3-gun and, in fact, has often been referred to as a World Championship match," Johnson said. "It tests more than just standing and shooting, including physical challenges, as well as mental ones. JP RM3G is unique and fun. It's a match that tests the well-roundedness of the shooter in the most unique setting in the world."

AR15.com-Rockcastle Pro-Am 3-Gun Championship

In 2011, arguably no 3-gun match received more hype, and no match was more anticipated, than the debut of the AR15.com-Rockcastle Pro-Am 3-Gun Championship. And with good reason, as, for the first time, internet forum juggernaut ARFCOM (AR15.com's nickname) provided massive support for a major match. Using its massive reach, word quickly spread about the first true Pro-Amateur 3-gun match.

Also contributing to the buzz was the venue, the Rockcastle Shooting Center, in Park City, Kentucky, a recreational resort that has quickly established itself as a premiere shooting venue. With approximately 2,000 acres of natural, rolling terrain, the Rock has the ability to put on a match that very few facilities can equal. Combined with its sporting clays, archery, golf, hotel, and restaurant and bar, the Rock provides the most unique shooting experience in the country, regardless the

discipline. Better yet, the Rock excels at hosting 3-gun matches, with the template already well established from hosting the Blue Ridge Mountain 3-Gun for several years, along with specialty events such as the Pan American IPSC Shotgun Championship in 2010.

Once the idea was established, NRA Board Member Joe DeBergalis, Rockcastle owners, brothers Nick and Nate Noble, industry leaders such as Brownells' CEO Pete Brownell, and, of course, the Avila family, who own and operate ARFCOM, began casting their wide net in search for industry support. The result was overwhelming, with pro clinics, side matches, and one of the richest Outlaw prize tables in the support, not to mention a second, separate match designed exclusively for amateur 3-gun competitors, many of whom had never competed in any shooting discipline at any level. Veteran 3-gunner Jeff Cramblit was brought in to create the format itself, and the result was two unique matches, one a challenging open course of fire for top 3-gun competitors; the other a slightly scaled back version, one where competitors with limited experience could still expect to successfully finish the match.

The matches themselves turned out to be entertaining ones, with the usual suspects dominating the top of the Pro match, while the Amateur match enabled a completely different set of shooters a moment in the spotlight. Ultimately, Daniel Horner dominated, Jerry Miculek survived, and Corey Schwanz held on by the slimmest of margins—three completely different ends to a remarkable weekend at the inaugural AR15.com-Rockcastle Pro-Am 3-Gun Championships.

In the Pro Tactical division, Horner (768.00) dominated a field of more than 170 competitors, winning five of eight stages on his way to the overall win. Taran Butler (719.36) finished second, followed by Kelly Neal (660.08), Chris Sechiatano (639.53), and Keith Garcia (638.73).

In the Open class, Jerry Miculek survived a tough back-and-forth battle with Clint Upchurch, James Darst, Mike Voigt, and Tony Holmes—all of which were in the hunt at some time to win the match. Miculek's 709.88 points secured the Open win, followed by Upchurch (679.61), Darst (660.32), Voigt (649.17), and Holmes (633.89).

On the Amateur side, Corey Schwanz (572.85) survived a nail-biter over Lee Pettross (570.05), winning by a mere 2.8 match points. Chris Cazin (564.67) took third, followed by David Schuster (563.42) and Patrick Kangeter (541.01).

"After looking at the scores for five of the seven stages, I knew it would be close," said Schwanz, who's a reloading technician for Sinclair International, a Brownells company. "I had been shooting fairly well, but after what happened to me on the final stage of the weekend, I thought I had lost too much time. I was surprised to hear my name called as the top amateur shooter."

Cramblit and his staff designed two separate matches,

with eight Pro stages and seven Amateur stages. However, they shared one common theme in that they were wide open. With relatively fast par times, most of the stages were fairly short in round count, as well, and required minimal movement compared to other natural terrain courses of fire. All combined to keep plenty of brass in the air, as well as smiles on the faces of the competitors.

"I liked the open stages of this match," Schwanz said. "Most of them had a variety of ways to shoot them, and we had to figure out what would be the best way for us. It fit with what I like to do in matches—try to find the shot or angle no one else saw and gain some time because of it."

The match format, which effectively served as two simultaneous matches, enabled approximately 350 shooters to compete over the three-day event. While the format itself was unique, with this Pro-Am being the first of its kind in the sport of 3-gun, the event also borrowed heavily from other successful firearm industry events to create a stellar weekend. Several companies provided support personnel and kicked in prizes for fun and challenging side shoots that ran throughout the weekend. Arguably, even more popular were the pro clinics, where top 3-gun competitors such as Bruce Piatt, Bennie Cooley, Jerry Miculek, and others held free clinics on different aspects of shooting 3-gun competitions.

"It seemed like everybody who was anybody in 3-gun was at this match and sponsored a side match," said Pro Match competitor Karla Herdzik. "Benelli sponsored a shotgun speed shoot. FNH had a P90 machine gun

stake shoot. Crimson Trace had a pistol run through one of Rockcastle's infamous pitch-black caves. LaRue Tactical was there with its new OBR (Optimized Battle Rifle), and its famous barbecue trailer! And there was a 3-man team stake shoot, too! The best part of all these side matches? All the proceeds went to benefit some great charities supporting the men and women who sacrifice their lives daily for our freedoms—the NRA Life of Duty Foundation, the Lone Survivor Foundation, and Task Force Dagger."

"The event in general was a blast," Schwantz said. "This was my first trip to Rockcastle and my first national-level 3-gun match. I really liked the Pro-Am format and the multiple days of shooting. The pro clinics were a great addition to the schedule, as well. The level of support this match received from all the sponsors was absolutely amazing. All of them deserve a big thank you!"

"The great folks of AR15.com, Rockcastle Shooting Center, Brownells, Sinclair, the PoliceStore.com, and Hornady joined in our mission to open up this competition to more competitors than ever before," said NRA Board Member and Match Chairman Joe DeBergalis. "Our event was unique and original in format. The emphasis was to provide an avenue for those wanting to become active within 3-gun, while simultaneously providing a challenging event for the seasoned competitor. Our Match Director, Jeff Cramblit, accomplished that task admirably. Our team at the Rockcastle Shooting Center, led by the Noble Family and General Jerry Humble (USMC, Ret.), did a good job ensuring that our facilities were in superb shape. Everyone was touched by their generous hospitality. As an NRA Board Member, I received great support from Wayne LaPierre, the NRA's executive vice president, and Chris Cox of the NRA's Institute for Legislative Action. We also introduced the NRA's Life of Duty Program, a mission-driven NRA initiative that benefited our acknowledged charities, the Task Force Dagger Foundation and the Lone Survivor Foundation. There was a vendors' row and demonstration area for our participating sponsors that enabled those competing and

The ARFCOM-Rockcastle Pro-Am utilized the Rockcastle Shooting Center's Cowboy Town for one of its 3-gun stages.

watching the opportunity to try the very same equipment and gear the competitors used during the match.

"We created an 'industry buy-in,' by inviting our friends in the industry to take stock in the match and enable us to provide for them a showcase of their products that could help grow the sport," DeBergalis continued. "For instance, we provided range access to those companies that wanted to display their products in real time. Our side matches allowed interested parties the opportunity to try LaRue Tactical, Spikes Tactical, FNH USA, CMMG, Crimson Trace, Bushnell, Benelli, and JP products, to name a few, during range conditions that allowed them instant point-of-sale opportunities. This

also allowed for instant branding and product recognition—much like the NASCAR adage, 'Race on Sunday, buy on Monday.' Well, based on the feedback from our participating sponsors, everyone there took that to heart!"

As word began to spread about the Pro-Am inaugural match, more and more companies decided get involved. For some, it marked their first entry into the sport of 3-gun.

"We are proud to say that we opened opportunities in 3-gun for those companies who had not yet been involved. Daniel Defense, Troy Industries, Alexander Arms, CMC Triggers, and Ritchie Leather were all first-time sponsors who had a great time and have already committed again for next year," DeBergalis said.

"Through the hard work and effort of all involved, we enjoyed welcoming a total of 61 sponsors to our event and team. And, when I use the word 'team,' I mean it. As I mentioned previously, their buy-in was integral to our success. Most importantly, each sponsor became a major part of the competition and now has a stake in the growth of our match for next year.

The Pro-Am delivered a home run on a scale seldom seen in any type of first-year match, a testament to the tremendous cast of supporters involved, and the Rock as the pivotal cog in the wheel. To that end, the online registration process took a matter of minutes for the follow-on match this year, with an initial waiting list numbering in the

hundreds! It's fair to say the Pro-Am is here to stay on the Outlaw 3-gun circuit.

Ozark 3-Gun Championship

In 2009, following on the heels of successful new match introductions such as the DPMS Tri-Gun Challenge, Fort Benning 3-Gun Challenge, and the Midwest 3-Gun Challenge, another new major Outlaw match debuted in Missouri—the Ozark 3-Gun Championship (O3GC). Taking advantage of leased rural land near Columbia, the Ozark immediately became known for its rolling natural terrain and the good stage design woven in.

"The Ozark 3-Gun Championship is a natural terrain match shot in the hills of the Ozarks, in southern Missouri," said Kirk

Broyles, match director, prior to the 2010 event. "It features fun and challenging stages for all levels of competitors. And now we have a new location with more than 1,000 acres at our disposal. There are some great stages."

Challenging long-range rifle stages, a tremendous amount of small, reactive steel pistol targets, and a massive all-shotgun stage have become signature at Ozark. With the second venue in 2011, a small lake enabled the added dimensions of rifle shooting from unstable platforms,

Rafael Esqueda takes on rifle targets during the 2011 AR15.com-Rockcastle Pro-Am 3-Gun at the Rockcastle Shooting Center in Park City, Kentucky.

The Ozark 3-Gun Championship is one of several major matches trending toward the use of small, knock-over steel for pistol targets.

such as a small boat. Also in 2011, Ozark was held on the weekend of September 11, the 10-year anniversary of the 2001 terrorist attacks. An active-duty soldier himself, Broyles dedicated the match to the memory of that horrific day, and every stage was themed after important battles or missions conducted by U.S. forces in the War on Terror.

Since 2010, Ozark has been a 3GN-Affiliated match, hosting two 3GN Shoot-Offs and now part of the 3GN Outlaw Division series, giving yet more reasons to shoot one of the top matches in Outlaw 3-gun.

"I'm very excited to be a part of *3-Gun Nation*. It's doing great things to promote the sport," Broyles said last season. "As the newest match of this size, I am extremely honored to host the first 3GN Shoot-Off of the 2011 season. And I look forward to a long, successful relationship."

FNH USA 3-Gun Championship

One of three new matches to debut in 2011, the FNH USA 3-Gun Championship didn't receive quite the hype as the Pro-Am, when the shooting season unfolded. This was understandable, as the Pro-Am had launched a completely new format and was publicized to the hilt on AR15.COM. FNH, mean-

while, quietly went to work delivering what the East Coast had never had—a premiere, major 3-gun match of its very own.

Rather than re-invent the wheel, as the Pro-Am had, FNH USA match director Larry Houck sought to perfect it. His vision was realized in an interesting blend of range bay and natural terrain courses of fire. The stages were constructed in a wide-open fashion, yet the most interesting stage philosophy was one centered on "shooters' choice." On these, competitors had varying degrees of selection by which targets could be engaged with certain firearms. The result was a wonderful blend of fast shooting and wide-ranging strategy, along with some demanding and technical mid- and long-range rifle shooting thrown in for good measure. Ultimately, for many who competed, the FNH USA 3-Gun Championship was the surprise hit of the 3-gun season.

"As a competitor, I love to have choices," Houck said. "It's no fun traveling to matches where everyone has to shoot a stage the same way. I also wanted competitors to play to their strengths. If you're better with a pistol than a shotgun, then shoot your pistol. No competitor can look back and say the stage caused them not to do well. Even more interesting, a tremendous amount of rain leading up to the match prevented us from getting all of the bays completed. So it actually made our match better, as we had a true mixture of ranges and natural terrain on which to shoot."

The match also marked the debut for one of our country's newest range and training facilities. Sprawling across a vast expanse of West Virginia mountains, the new Peacemaker National Training Center, while early in its development, provided opportunities not available at a standard square-bay type range facility.

"This was the facility's first big match, so it was a huge learning curve and at a rapid pace, considering I was doing all the coordination from 1,900 miles away," Houck said. "The staff were great to work with, and I can only see better things in the future for Peacemaker National Training Center."

One of the highlights of the event was the unique use of FN firearms. Used as stage guns, with all ammunition provided by FN, the event gave competitors an opportunity to shoot products they might not ever have the chance to otherwise.

"We shot a PS90, suppressed SCAR 16, and an FN 303 Less Lethal Launcher," Houck said. "Most people will *never* get to shoot these guns, especially the Less Lethal Launcher, as it's not available to the general public."

Ultimately, the inaugural FNH USA 3-Gun Championship was a huge success, setting it up to be yet another must-shoot event.

"Expect exciting stages with choices," Houck said. "We want to make this a great experience for everyone involved, from the shooter to the range staff and especially our sponsors. We want to be the match that everyone wants to be involved with."

Robby Johnson takes on pistol targets placed among the trees during a stage setup in the woods at the Blue Ridge Mountain 3-Gun.

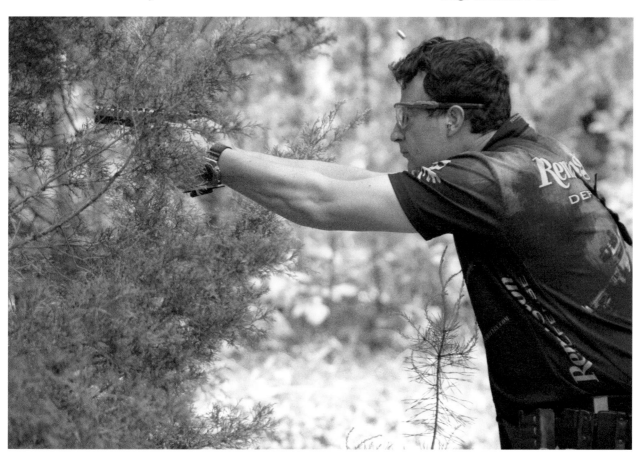

Blue Ridge Mountain 3-Gun

From the very beginnings at Big Bear, the driving force behind much of the innovation in major practical shooting competition has come out of the western United States. However, in 2008, Andy Horner founded the Blue Ridge Mountain 3-Gun Championship (BRM3G), giving the sport, at the time, only its second major 3-gun event east of the Mississippi.

"The BRM3G was begun in order to bring a major 3-gun championship to the eastern U.S.," said Horner, match director of the BRM3G. "With all of the matches except the Fort Benning 3-Gun Challenge (now defunct) being west of the Mississippi, there are many shooters who have not been exposed to the excitement of high-level 3-gun competition. Being able to talk with, watch, and compete against the best shooters in the world is introducing new shooters to 3-gun and is increasing interest in our sport generally."

While the eastern states may have been slow to develop major 3-gun competitions, Blue Ridge Mountain nevertheless hit the ground running under the watchful eye of match director Andy Horner, a veteran multi-gun shooter. Taking lessons learned from competing in major matches all over the United States, Blue Ridge utilizes a remarkable expanse of land at the new Rockcastle Shooting Center, near Bowling Green, Kentucky. As such, Blue Ridge utilizes the natural terrain features of Kentucky's western foothills, in turn delivering what are some of the most challenging stage designs in 3-gun competition.

While I haven't competed in every major out there, of the ones I've personally shot, the Blue Ridge has been my favorite thus far. For the same reason some top pros *don't* like the Blue Ridge, I think others are drawn to it. Physically demanding and technically challenging, the stages at Blue Ridge challenge equally with all three guns, while the venue itself provides a wild card. Targets are hidden behind trees, in bright sunlight one moment and then in contrasting shade the next—you *never* know what you will see at BRM3G. While some 3-gunners understandably prefer the challenge be equally applied to all at all times, I still think there is

Match director Andy Horner is famous for his challenging target placements—and sometimes hard-to-see unpainted steel—at the Blue Ridge Mountain 3-Gun.

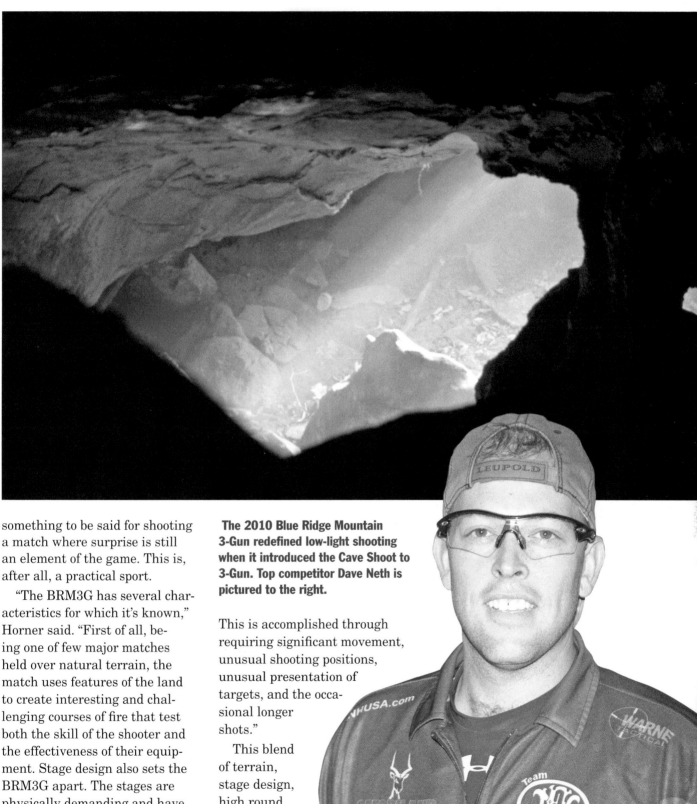

The 2010 Blue Ridge Mountain 3-Gun redefined low-light shooting when it introduced the Cave Shoot to 3-Gun. Top competitor Dave Neth is pictured to the right.

something to be said for shooting a match where surprise is still an element of the game. This is, after all, a practical sport.

"The BRM3G has several characteristics for which it's known," Horner said. "First of all, being one of few major matches held over natural terrain, the match uses features of the land to create interesting and challenging courses of fire that test both the skill of the shooter and the effectiveness of their equipment. Stage design also sets the BRM3G apart. The stages are physically demanding and have a higher than average round count—this is *not* a stand-and-shoot match. We strive to create stages that require competitors to get out of their comfort zone and have their abilities tested.

This is accomplished through requiring significant movement, unusual shooting positions, unusual presentation of targets, and the occasional longer shots."

This blend of terrain, stage design, high round count, and demanding match tempo have instantly elevated Blue

Ridge to major status, one of only about 10 matches in the country to create such demand. In only a few short years, the competitor field, comprised of novice and veteran shooters alike, has grown exponentially,

"We have definitely been growing," Horner said prior to Blue Ridge 2010. "The first year we had 99 shooters, then 176, and this year the match is full and expecting 240-plus shooters."

While the Blue Ridge Mountain 3-Gun delivers an uncommon shooting experience, with a top-notch match, resort hotel and other amenities all in one location, what keeps the pros from all over the country coming back is the high-octane match itself.

"Again, the BRM3G is not a stand-and-shoot match," Horner emphasized. "Some folks love that type, some don't. Fortunately, 3-gun matches around the country each have their own flavor, and the BRM3G provides an opportunity for those who enjoy a more physical and technical match."

Fallen Brethren 3-Gun

The final new major 3-gun event to debut in 2011 was developed in an attempt to fill the hole in the match calendar voided by the demise of one of the top matches in the country—the Fort Benning 3-Gun Challenge. While the match had been continuously full, the prize table loaded, and the shooting always top notch under the watchful eye of the U.S. Army Marksmanship Unit Action Shooting Team, the match nevertheless was cancelled, apparently a decision by higher ranking officials.

After a group of soldiers sought to continue the match tradition at a new venue, the task

fell to Jim Smith at Spartan Tactical, a private training academy outside of Dallas, Texas. Smith built his staff, picked up the sword, and eventually brought in Sheldon Carruth and his team from Texas Multi-Gun for additional staffing and support. This proved to be a key move, and the result was a well-run, challenging course of fire over distinctive, Texas brush country natural terrain. Despite rain, fog, and extremely challenging footing at times, approximately 150 soaked and muddy competitors shot an entire 10-stage major match in 48 hours, and there likely wasn't a disappointed shooter in the bunch.

While several days of rain dictated a slower pace on many stages, making footing a challenge across the immense 10,000-acre facility, solid stage design and a strong crew of range staff pushed the field through the entire match in just two days. True, FB3G enjoyed a bit of luck, with a reduced field of 150 competitors, but completing such a match in just two days is virtually unheard of and a testament to the staff running this event.

For those who braved the elements, the payoff was an outstanding course of fire, highlighted by Stage 9, a long-range rifle course that required competitors to shoot from the side of a cliff down into a panoramic valley below to engage rifle steel at approximately 100 to 550 yards. This stage demanded calculation of angles of fire, calling the wind, and multiple target holds for a good run. In the Tactical Optics division, Kelly Neal outpaced Rustin Bernskoetter 824.46 to 791.03 to pick up the win. Burton Thompson (776.20), Adam Popplewell (750.74), and

Trip McIngvale (743.14) rounded out the top five.

Chuck Anderson narrowly edged out Tony Holmes 816.48 to 810.41 to win the Open division. Anderson put together a solid match, shooting early with the match staff on Thursday. However, Holmes almost certainly delivered the more impressive performance, battling adverse weather conditions, yet still commanding two stage wins on the final day. Holmes won Stages 2 and 3, after shooting them in their absolute worst conditions, an impressive feat. James Darst (759.41) finished third, followed by Jesse Tischauser (666.43) and Kelly Raglin (579.17).

In the Heavy Metal Optics race, Tate Moots announced his definitive return to 3-gun with an impressive victory, winning seven stages and scoring 886.85 match points. (Moots has competed in very few matches over the last two seasons while recovering from a back injury.) J.P. Gangl (726.49) finished second, followed by J.J. Johnson (653. 63), Vance Blackwell (556.56) and Shane Cuperus (437.13).

Kuan Watson (846.72) outlasted West Chandler (782.13) to win the Tactical Iron division. Michael Chambers (677.96) finished third, followed by Ben Zacharias (591.67) and Jeremy Moore (579.04).

As impressive as the top shooters were and despite the bad weather, the most notable feature to this first edition of the newly organized FB3G was the backdrop itself, Spartan Tactical. Run by former Army Special Forces operator Jim Smith, Spartan's massive natural terrain facility enabled gunsmith and range master Sheldon Carruth tremendous creativity in stage and course design. Major match sponsors Remington, Leupold, and DSG Arms, along with secondary sponsors Warne Scope Mounts, SureFire, XRAIL, Stag Arms, MGM Targets, and many more, contributed a solid prize table for a first-year event, one that promises to grow into a must-shoot event on the major match Outlaw 3-gun circuit.

USPSA Multi-Gun Nationals

The term "Outlaw 3-Gun" exists in overt defiance to what some in 3-gun believe USPSA represents. To be fair, much of the early work in Outlaw 3-gun grew in an absence of USPSA rules and definitions, as the pistol doctrine didn't always work for this emerging multi-gun sport. However, compared to all but a few of the major matches currently in operation, USPSA Multi-Gun Nationals has been doing it longer than most, and that deserves credit. And, while USPSA has its detractors, there is also a staunch, loyal following of competitors that travel the country to compete, officiate, and set-up USPSA events, including the Multi-Gun Nationals. As such, for some especially die-hard, high-level USPSA pistol competitors, USPSA Multi-Gun Nationals remains one of the top venues in the sport, a must-attend match on the national major 3-gun circuit.

In recent years, much has been made of the stage design at Nationals. To many veteran competitors, after years of lackluster opinions of the match, recent stage design has improved, elevating this event's stature. Under the watchful eye of former president Mike Voigt, a very vocal supporter of multi-gun within USPSA, the Multi-Gun Nationals

have indeed flourished in recent years. Today, USPSA is under fresh leadership, with newly elected president Phil Strader. A pistol competitor by trade, Strader nonetheless competes in 3-gun, as well, and, in fact, qualified for the 3GN Championship Finale, in 2012. What remains to be seen is how hard Strader will push for the continued development of USPSA 3-gun.

The Other Players

Shooting a major 3-gun event is a large commitment in time and money. Match fees are usually somewhere around $250. Add in travel costs, meals, and enough ammunition to get you through the match, and a major shoot can easily run a couple thousand dollars to attend.

"There is an enormous amount of time and energy that goes into training, preparing, and actually attending the matches," said Team FNH USA's Dianna Liedorff, who finished second in the 2011 3-Gun Nation Ladies Division. "The matches are pretty tricky to get into and require a lot of planning relatively early in the season. By February, I was already entered into every major 3-gun match I planned on attending for the year."

"For me, the time commitment is the biggest obstacle to overcome," said Open division shooter Clint Upchurch. "Having a full-time job, a family, and other priorities makes the preparation, training, and travel required to be at the top of the sport extremely difficult. There is a lot of time spent prepping gear, loading ammo, and training before you even talk about spending four to five days to travel and compete at an event. Trying to balance these factors without

neglecting other priorities seems almost impossible at times."

"There's a lot of gear and ammo required, and if you don't drive, you have to figure out the most economical way to get it there," Liedorff continued. "That requires a lot of planning. If I'm not driving, I've had friends that are driving take my stuff while I fly. Or I plan ahead with ammo and leave my bag/ammo on the FNH USA truck. Most major matches are three days long. That's a huge commitment of time away from work."

Luckily, there are several of what I like to call "regionals" across the country. While that's not an official designation, it does give a description for matches that are obviously larger in size, scale, and cost than a local club match, yet more affordable and more easily accessible than a major.

Compared to 250 shooters at a major, regionals run 100 shooters or more. Instead of a $200,000 prize table, there will be a much more modest selection of guns and gear to be won. The real prize here, most often, is in the shooting itself.

From Fort Smith, Arkansas, to Kentucky State in Owensboro, to USPSA Area 1 Multi-Gun in Parma, Idaho, some of the finest one- and two-day match schedules in 3-gun can be found at venues of this size.

For an affordable price, and within driving distance to where you live, chances are there is a once-a-year regional-type 3-gun event. If you're not quite ready to make the jump to a major 3-gun event, but want something more than your local club has to offer, a regional 3-gun match has the potential to really deliver a fantastic experience.

DIVI

Yamil R. Sued photo

CHAPTER 5.

THE DIVISIONS

I n the sport of 3-gun, available equipment encompasses a wide range, one with a vast spectrum of performance capabilities. Race guns in light calibers and loaded down for softer recoil perform entirely differently than full-power .308 rifles and .45-caliber pistols with military ball loads. As such, competing head-to-head with such diverse equipment is not a fair comparison.

Over the years, several different equipment divisions have been established and, for the most part, even standardized across Outlaw 3-gun matches. From the fast, accessory-driven Open division to the pounding big-bore guns in the Heavy Metal division, 3-gun's different equipment divisions are really a big part of what attracts shooters into the game and what sets it apart from other shooting disciplines.

Tactical Optics

By an overwhelming margin, often exceeding 75 percent or more at major 3-gun matches, Tactical Optics is the division in which most competitors play. Not only does it have the greater number of shooters by volume, but the majority of the very best of the talent pool play here. Daniel Horner, Taran Butler, Greg Jordan, Tyler Payne, Rustin Bernskoetter, and many other of the best 3-gunners in the sport call Tactical Optics home at every event in which they compete.

"The Tactical Optics division, casually referred to as 'Tac Scope' by many who play the game, also goes by the monikers 'Scoped Tactical' and 'Limited Scoped,'" said Patrick Kelley. "This is the division where the majority of competitors play, and for good reason. The equipment roster reads virtually word-for-word the same as it does for the Limited division, with the exception being your rifle optic choices. Whereas in the Limited division you are held to a magnification maximum of 1X for your scope (i.e., iron sight and/or red dot), in Tactical Optics, you can run any scope you desire. And many desire more power!"

For the most part, it's the allowance of the variable power scope, while still limiting the exceedingly expensive accessories that define the Open class, that maintains Tactical Optics as the standard bearer. That scope use, for the most part, is simply driven by the challenges competitors commonly face now, with targets, often within the same stage, varying in distance from a few feet to 400 yards or more.

"Over the course of a season, shooters will face targets on the long side of 400 yards," Kelley

explained. "Some match directors take it a bit further, challenging and perhaps frustrating competitors with engagements to 600 yards. Couple this with tough lighting conditions, wind, and weather, and having a 4X, 6X, or even an 8X scope on top of your rifle makes sense."

As such, the new breed of variable power scopes, with power ranges that begin at 1X or 1.5X and range past 4X and on up to even 8X, dominate the field. Leupold, Swarovski, Bushnell, Burris, and more all make rifle scopes within this niche. Designed with an eye toward military and law enforcement use, the 1X variable revolution has totally redefined what once was a division in which a 1-4X scope (of which many are still used effectively), previously dominated the equipment choices among the consistent match winners.

The gun platforms themselves are quite wide ranging, with no one brand leading the pack, but there are certain types that see more use than others. In rifles, AR-15s chambered in .223/5.56

are king. Stag Arms and Colt's now both offer out-of-the-box rifles ready for 3-gun, competing with those from JP Rifles and DPMS. DoubleStar is currently planning a dedicated 3-gun rifle, while Samson Manufacturing is rumored to be working on an entry, as well. FNH USA's model SCAR 16 has made a big splash, in large part due to the solid use by its own team members in competition. It's now becoming common place to see SCARs in rifle racks at major matches that don't belong to Team FNH USA

shooters, evidence of the gun gaining acceptance.

The most widely used shotgun among top shooters is most likely the Benelli M2, though the FNH USA SLP has made a major impact over the last couple of seasons and become a serious threat to Benelli's dominating presence in the sport. Mossberg's 930 has also seen some use since its debut, as has the VersaMax creation from Remington.

Pistols, like rifles, are really all over the place, even if the majority of veteran pistol shoot-

(left and top) During the Heavy Metal divison run at the 2011 Kentucky State Multi-Gun Championships Bryan Ray runs a single-stack 1911 on the pistol stage, and loads his pump-action Benelli Nova during shotgun action. This top competitor is shown dialing up his elevation knob on his Springfield M1A while competing in the Heavy Metal division at the 2011 Blue Ridge Mountain 3-Gun (bottom).

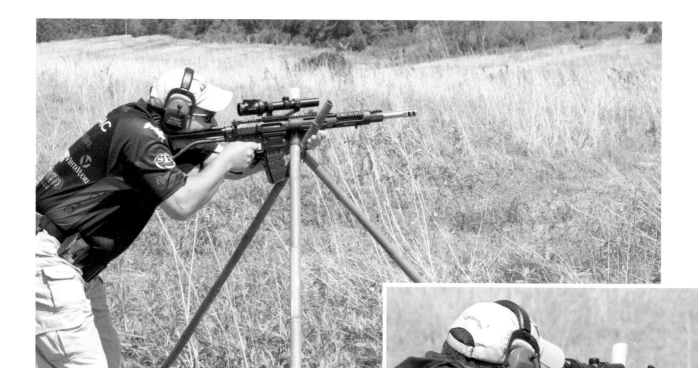

Tom Carpenter, competing in Tactical Optics, engages long-range rifle targets from shooting sticks, as required during a stage at the 2011 Blue Ridge Mountain 3-Gun.

ers do use some form of the 2011 (yes, that's 2011, not 1911), most often an STI or Caspian build. But Glocks, Springfield XDs, Smith & Wesson M&Ps, and even the new FNH USA Model FNS are also popular choices among competitors.

"The overall equipment is virtually the same as one would use in the Limited division," Kelley said. "There will be an AR in .223/5.56, a self-loading shotgun in 12-gauge, and a pistol holding 18 or more rounds in either 9mm or .40-caliber. There are no comps, ports, or optics allowed on your pistol or shotgun. In the Tactical Optics division, you just bolt your favorite scope onto your rifle and you're ready to rock."

Ultimately, the Tactical Optics division really just represents the types of firearms that have the most widespread appeal

across the greatest number of competitors. Affordable, easy to use, and with many dual-role purposes, Tactical Optics firearms and gear are most assuredly the products that best define the sport of 3-gun and those who shoot it.

"This is the division where most shooters start and stay," Kelley said. "The equipment is practical in size and weight and, as configured, are useful for other operations. Need a varmint whacker? Got it. Upland gun? Plug your shotgun's mag tube and you'll have a fast handling pellet spreader. Pistol for personal protection? Why not? Any of the battery of three could well defend hearth and home. Now *that's* practical. Heck,

maybe that's what it ought to be called—the *Practical* division!"

It's also the division where the top pros in the sport come to play. The 2012 3GN Pro Series marks the first year where all 3GN Series points—reserved for the shooters at the top level— will be earned exclusively in Tactical Optics. A television move, as well as a competitive one, the Tactical Optics-only format will once and for all settle the question as to who are the absolute top competitors in the game.

In years past, the sport crowned champions at each indi-

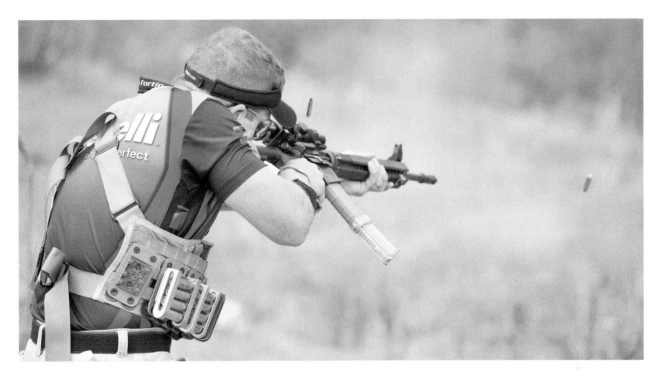

Ben Fortin, shooting in Tactical Optics, uses his Dueck Defense RTS sights to engage short-range targets at the 2011 Rocky Mountain 3-Gun.

vidual event in several different equipment divisions. This is a system that remains intact at Outlaw matches, as it should, but to mainstream America, this is analogous to putting NASCAR, Formula One, and Truck Series drivers, each running their different cars, all on the same track at the same time. So the 3GN Pro Series format finally puts and keeps all the top shooters in one division, going head-to-head, to determine individual match winners and crown a season champion. Regardless the division's name, putting the very best shooters in the world together, competing heads-up for the largest cash payouts in the sport, will be unquestionably exciting and may be just the spark 3-gun needs to elevate it even further into the limelight.

Open Division

In 3-gun, the Open division is just that—the no-holds-barred, anything goes, brass-in-the-air, high-speed division of practical shooting. Watching Jerry Miculek, Mike Voigt, or Clint Upchurch absolutely burn down a stage in this type of class is a sight to behold.

By comparison, all other divisions are ones that limit, in varying degrees, the firearms and gear. As such, the Open division is more gear-driven than any other, with a high emphasis placed on ammunition capacity and muzzle control. Increased capacity reduces time-robbing reloads, and highly modified compensators keep the muzzle flat, thereby increasing control and speed—the Open shooter lays on the trigger and lets it rip.

"Open looked like the most fun division," said Colt's Clint Upchurch, describing why he chose the Open division, when switching from USPSA pistol competition to 3-gun two years ago. "Having so many options

with the gear was appealing, and I thought it would be a more natural transition into 3-gun after a few years of exclusively shooting Open pistol."

In Open, high-capacity magazines—from SureFire 60-rounders on up the 100-round Beta-C mag—are used for running rifles. As it is in all divisions, .223-chambered ARs rule the day here, except that restrictions concerning muzzle brakes and compensator sizes go out the window. Bipods are also used to good effect in Open.

Open is also the division that allows multiple optics on rifles. Companies such as Warne Scope Mounts, with its RAMP mount, produce mounting solutions that provide for a traditional variable power scope on top of the rifle, while also incorporating a 1X reflex sight mounted 45 degrees from the scope and in line with the bore. The set-up enables shooters to sight the 1X for close-range paper targets, anywhere from 10 to 25 yards, while the main scope is used to engage (top and left) Tommy Thacker runs his XRAIL-equipped SLP in the Open division at the 2011 Rocky Mountain 3-Gun, and rapidly engages pistol targets with an Open handgun during the 2011 Superstition Mountain Mystery 3-Gun.

(below) Tony Holmes runs an XRAIL-integrated Benelli in the Open division at the 2011 Rocky Mountain 3-Gun.

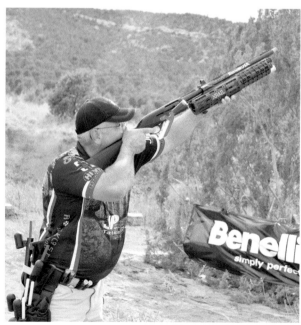

(above) Though he sometimes uses an XRAIL in competition, Jerry Miculek used only an extended magazine tube and speedloaders on his Open shotgun, during the 2010 Midwest 3-Gun Championship.

long-range targets. The combination, one now being copied by elite U.S. military units, delivers incredibly fast target acquisition at close range, while maintaining increased power setting for long-range engagement.

"My experience has been that you lose or gain the most ground in long-range rifle," Upchurch explained. "There is just more time to be wasted when you take a lot of extra shots with the rifle. Also, wind and lighting are more of a factor here. If you shoot shotgun and pistol under different conditions, those things won't make a big difference, but they can change things tremendously for the rifle."

Open pistols are almost universally of the 2011 configuration, with STI, Caspian, Infinity, and more showing up in high-speed holsters at major matches. Capacity is high, red dot optics are allowed, comps are huge, and any other manner of gunsmithing and accessories are used to squeeze the final bit of speed out of this 100-year-old 1911 design.

"A pistol can be anything you wish, so long as it's 9x19mm or larger," Patrick Kelley said. "Magazine *length*, not capacity, is restricted to 170 millimeters. Port it, comp it, hang crystals from the rearview mirror. If that makes you go faster, it's all good. Bolt on any sight system with the exception of projecting lasers. Kickstands and gas pedals are okay, too! Really! A kickstand, in this instance, is an arm sticking off the side of the pistol that props it up so you can get a better grip for those lying-flat-on-the-table starts. Gas pedals? Nope, not kidding, this speed part is for your support hand thumb to press down on and help control muzzle lift!"

Then there's the shotgun. In terms of pistols and rifle, it's mainly just different variations on the same theme that make up the primary differences in competitors' gear. Shotguns, on the other hand, are quite different, and they provide the one place within the Open division where individual preference makes its loudest expression.

"The difference from Limited to Open shotguns is in magazine capacity and the use of electronic sights and speedloaders," said Bruce Piatt. "A shooter can take his Limited shotgun, put a longer mag tube on it, install a bolt-on Armstec speedloader, mount a Burris SpeedBead, screw in a combination compensator/choke, and be ready to shoot Open—all without permanently modifying his gun."

"The Open division shotgun displays the biggest departure from the other divisions," Kelley said. "Whereas speedloaders are forbidden in all other divisions, in Open, these devices, including detachable box magazines, are virtually *obligatory*! An Open division shooter *could* live without comps, optics, or porting, but one would be hard-pressed to win without the ability to speedload the shotgun!"

Today, shotgun speedloaders come in three basic forms, stick types, detachable box magazines, and a singular product called the XRAIL, which is a self-articulating, rotary magazine tube system. At this point, it's hard to say which style is more effective, as each of the most consistent top shooters in 3-gun use a different shotgun speedloader system.

Clint Upchurch, winner of the 2011 3GN Open division, runs an R&R Saiga, a highly customized, box magazine-fed shotgun sys-

tem. Meanwhile, Mike Voigt, who Upchurch narrowly edged out, runs a traditional stick speedloader, as does Jerry Miculek. Miculek has also been experimenting with an XRAIL system in competition, the same system used by top Open shooters James Darst, a 3GN Shoot-Off winner, and Tony Holmes.

If you want to shoot in Open, you had either be heavily sponsored or have a heavy wallet, as Open gear is quite often the most expensive in the sport, especially the high-end race pistols that can exceed more than $4,000. An R&R Saiga shotgun can easily reach $3,500, while the XRAIL is pushing a $1,000 investment by the time you're completely geared up—and not including the shotgun itself. Thankfully, the rifle isn't that much more complicated than those used in most other divisions, though with high-end fore-ends, better barrels, and dual optics, you can still spend a lot of money here, too. For some, obviously, it's money well spent, and there is no denying the thrill of burning ammo at the rate so often enjoyed by 3-gun Open division shooters.

"If the guns of 3-gun were race cars, Open Division would be the home of the full-tilt, open-wheel F1 car," Kelley said. "While equipped with the latest go-fast parts, they can be a tuning nightmare, but in the right hands and running right, nothing is faster!"

Tactical Iron

Also known as "Tactical Limited" or "Limited," the 3-gun Tactical Iron division experienced a radical transformation during the 2011 season. A division (top and above) Team FNH USA's Larry Houck shoots off a legal Open division bipod during the 2011 Rocky Mountain 3-Gun, and he ran an XRAIL on his FN SLP shotgun while competing in the Open division at the same match.

(right) SureFire's Maggie Reese, geared up for the Open division, readies for a stage.

(below) SureFire's Maggie Resse takes on long-range rifle targets with her Open rifle, during a stage at the 2011 Rocky Mountain 3-Gun.

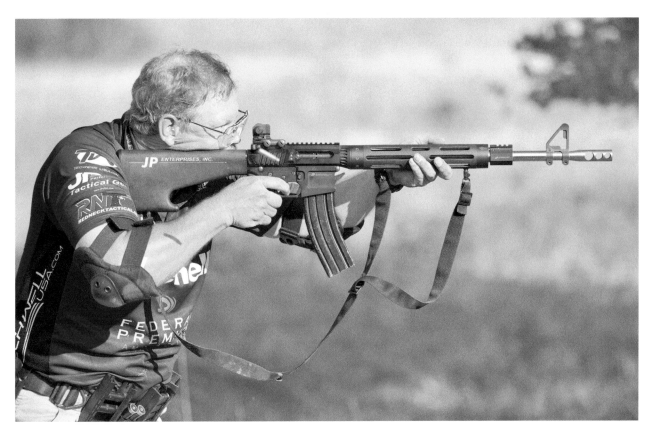

clearly in decline, as more and more competitors switched over to the popular Tactical Optics division, one simple rule change breathed new life into it—and kept alive a division that, in many ways, perpetuates as one of the more accessible divisions for new 3-gun shooters.

At the end of the 2010 season, a rumbling debate within the 3-gun community was gaining steam. It seemed a growing number of competitors were asking match directors to consider allowing 1X optics, i.e., non-magnified red dots or tubular sights, in the Tactical Iron division. Normally, any type of red dot or optic would automatically place a competitor in Tactical Optics.

"While Limited has been the domain of the iron sight shooter, many matches have adopted permissions for 1X or non-magnified electronic or optical sights," said Patrick Kelley. "This change has been, for the most part, welcomed by the 'old hand' iron sight shooters, not because they will change to optics, but because the addition of red dots or other optics with a maximum of 1X brings new blood to the division. Keep in mind that 1X power is what your eyes are when they're open."

Part of the argument for adding these limited sight accessories derived from the equipment list used by Tactical Optics and Open competitors. For years, both divisions had enjoyed the use of a secondary sighting system. In Open, competitors regularly use a 1X red dot as a secondary sight to a variable power optic. Mounted at 45 degrees from the main optic and in line with the bore, these optics are set up for 15- to 25-yard shots. In Tactical Optics, though, competitors have also long used iron sights as backup to a primary variable power scope. Like the red dots in Open,

Kurt Miller hammers close-range targets with his Tactical Iron rifle, during the 2011 Rocky Mountain 3-Gun.

in recent years it has become common practice to mount these irons at a 45-degree angle from the main tube and, again, in-line with the bore.

There were obvious parallels between the use of 1X optics and traditional iron sights already established in the sport, and a number of competitors felt that, if 1X optics could be used as a main sight, it could do much to help foster renewed interest in the Tactical Iron division, especially for older or other vision-challenged shooters. While a 1X optic has questionable overall advantages to irons, for those who can't pick up a front sight due to eyesight issue, the 1X means everything.

Many agreed, and the 2011 major matches across the country allowed competitors to use either a 1X optic or iron sights on their Tactical Iron division rifles. For some shooters, the move was controversial, for others a welcome change. Regardless, feedback was tremendous, and the division saw an immediate increase in participation levels across the board.

Ultimately, across the landscape of the major Outlaw 3-gun matches, both iron sight and 1X optic users did well. In fact, aside from a few new faces crashing the party, the top of the Tactical Iron division represented the usual suspects in 3-gun, proving once and for all its more about the skill of the shooter than the equipment he carries.

"It's funny, until last year, I was strongly of the opinion that I didn't want to shoot a rifle with a scope that wouldn't magnify up to at least 8X," said James Casanova, who finished second for the 2011 season in 3GN's Tactical Iron division. "Then, when I started to play with the 1X options out there, I began to realize how wrong I'd been about how the guys in this division were shooting.

"I had been of the opinion that, on the longer shots, out past 400 or so, they were just hosing the area until they hit something. I learned that was totally not true. It is a different kind of shooting for sure, but you can pick your shot and call your hit even with 1X. It's really satisfying to whack steel that looks like a pinhead in your sight picture.

"Now, there are some targets that are a bit tougher to score on, due to how those targets function. For instance, with a 1X, you can't see the bullet frag as it hits on some targets, so you do have to wait a little, but so does every

other non-magnified optics or iron sights shooter. On the plus side, the speed with which you can transition on shorter targets is excellent. Not having to think about what power I will shoot a stage with or where I plan to dial the scope are other advantages that make me smile. It's more about shooting and less about gear management on the clock."

"I personally like the feeling of accomplishment that comes from using iron sights," said Brian Vaught, who finished in the top 10 of the 3GN Tactical Iron Division using traditional iron sights. "No electronics, no fancy reticles, just knowing your rifle and how to hold on different sized targets at different ranges. When you hit a piece of steel that's way out there, it's worth the time you spent in preparation."

Clearly, both gear options have a place in the current Tactical Iron division. However, the choice of gear has ramifications well beyond bolting the accessory onto the rifle. Training regimen, shooting style, and even mental preparation to prepare for the upcoming sight picture are all affected by the choice of one's gear.

"My rear sight is a standard, bolt-on A2 aperture, made by Rock River," Vaught said. "The front is where individualism becomes apparent amongst iron shooters. I use a clamp-on JP A2-type gas block-mounted at the end of my barrel. My front post is a KNS 0.034. The JP base is solid as a rock, when clamped down, and having it mounted forward with the thin front post allows you to draw a fine bead on long-distance targets."

Iron sight shooters like Vaught typically mount the front sight as far forward as possible, increasing the sight radius between

the rear and front sights and maximizing accuracy potential at distance. Meanwhile, 1X optics users are free to run a lighter, more nimble rifle platform.

"Last year, I used the same rifle setup I would have if I'd shot Tactical Optics class, with the one difference being the Leupold Prismatic instead of a magnified scope," Casanova said. "The rifle was one of our builds for Carbon Arms, using a Firebird receiver set, a Nordic Components 16-inch stainless barrel with 1:8 rifling, an AR-Gold Trigger, Ace ARFX Stock, and a couple different comps over the season, including Henning's Thor .223, the Miculek comp, and an F2. Before the season got rolling and I was contemplating making the division switch to Limited/TI, I tested just about every red dot that fit the application. Then I got lucky, when my brother found a Prismatic on sale at the local Gander, and I figured, what the heck, let's give it a try.

"That Prismatic had the Circle Plex reticle in it, which is not ideal for this game," Casanova continued, "but of all the 1X options out there, I liked it the best. Then I heard that Kelly Neal—a veteran 3-gunner and top Tactical Iron competitor—was using the same scope with a different reticle. So, I contacted him, and he guided me toward the DCD reticle. I did give iron sights a try, but decided that, with the short amount of time I had to prep for the first match of the season, I didn't have time to set up a really good iron gun and get used to the sights. One of the really cool things about running the Prismatic is that barrel length becomes less of an issue, since sight radius is not part of the equation, plus you can swap the sight system back and forth between a magnified scope and the non-magnified without altering any other aspect of the rifle."

Most shooters were thrilled that non-magnified, 1X optics were allowed into Tactical Iron at major matches last year. But, as the 2011 3-gun season began to play out, it became clear that three distinctively different shooters might win the 3GN Tactical Iron Division, which is, effectively, the "Shooter of the Year" award for that specific division.

On one side was Kurt Miller, the legendary 3-gun veteran who had been competing in and running matches dating back to the days of the vaunted SOF match. Trying to knock off Miller were Kelly Neal, widely regarded as one of the most versatile competitors in the game, and James Casanova, who was having a major breakout year, in 2011.

If the personalities and competitors themselves didn't make for great storylines, the gear did. Both Neal and Casanova quickly took advantage of the new 1X rule, with each competitor running a Leupold Prismatic 1X (non-magnified) tubular scope. Meanwhile, Miller, the veteran who had shot iron sights for years, held onto traditional equipment. The debate was on— would Casanova and Neal have a gear advantage? Would it make a difference?

"Kurt and Kelly are both extremely good shooters and very seasoned competitors," Casanova said. "Kurt's preference for iron sights, I think, comes in part from being so in tune with the sight picture they give him over his years of working with them. He definitely proves that irons are not out of the picture in the

TI division. My impression of Kurt's shooting style is that he brings this knowledge with him to the line, and it shows through in the solid confidence he projects on every stage. The consistency of shooting the same sighting system for a long time gives Kurt the added advantage of not having to put conscious thought into his sight picture—his eyes know when things are right to let the round fly."

Casanova continued, "I haven't had the opportunity to shoot with Kelly much, so I really can't say I know anything about his shooting style, other than it's very effective. He was kind enough, when he had no idea who I was, to steer me in the right direction with the Prismatic reticle early in the season, so I am very grateful to him for that. The fact that Kelly has placed in the top three in every division at major matches over the last 10 years tells me that his fundamentals are rock solid, so it really doesn't matter what gear he's running, he'll be in the hunt. It may be partly because Kelly has shot so many different divisions in the past, his long experience has given him the itch to do something different in the form of running the Prismatic this year."

"You can't say that a guy like James or Kelly has an unfair advantage, because they would win no matter what equipment they shot," Vaught commented. "They are that good and have a strong game with all three guns. However, for those just starting off or coming up in the division, I believe the learning curve is a little less steep with a 1X optic than with true irons. I didn't like the addition of 1X at first, but it has expanded the

field of competitors, and the more shooters the better."

For new shooters interested in getting started in Tactical Iron, it's certainly not limited to just rifle shooting. Pistols and shotgun play just as an important role as they do in other divisions.

"I work mainly on sight focus," Casanova said, referring to his pistol practice. "What am I seeing with different kinds of shooting, and what am I getting as a result of what I am seeing? In 3-Gun, we get such a range of target types, sizes, and distances that having different sight/target focuses programmed so that they are sub-conscious is absolutely critical."

"Last year, my main focus was loading," Casanova said of his shotgun practice. "Over the winter, I worked on adapting a European style of loading two shells at a time, and developed with my brother and Mark Passamaneck a new shotshell caddie and clip system to support this loading method. Both products are now the core of our Carbon Arms TWinS loading system.

"I also put a good deal of effort into shooting slugs," Casanova told me. "I tested just about every make of slug I could get my hands on and found the ones that ran through my gun the best and were the most accurate. This year, I'm adding more shotgun shooting to my training in the form of sporting clays and other range drills."

This kind of fine-tuning aside, when it comes to the one key feature that sets the Tactical Iron division apart from all the rest, it is clearly the rifle.

"The pistol and shotgun are about the same as in other divisions," Vaught said. "If you want to shoot Tactical Iron, you really need to get out and shoot from some difficult positions and at the various ranges you're going to expect in a match. Know your holds out to 400 yards or so. Shoot some reactive targets out to 300 or 400 yards. Understand that the only way to confirm a 300-yard zero is to shoot your rifle at that distance. Don't let the first time you shoot at a

Kelly Neal, who finished second in the 2011 3GN Tactical Iron division, runs a stage during the 2011 Blue Ridge Mountain 3-Gun.

barely visible flasher be on the clock. When your squad gets to a stage and the targets are being painted, ask if you can shoot first. Every little bit helps."

Finding the right sighting option in Tactical Iron, for most competitors, will be through trial and error. Compared to the irons sights used by top competitors, the standard A2-type front sight post is too thick to reliably maintain the accuracy required at major matches. On the other

hand, all 1X optics are not created equal, with the reticle itself generally being the most important cog in the wheel. The only way for a competitor to know what suits them best is to get out and send rounds downrange with as many different sighting systems as possible.

"Get out and try every kind of 1X or iron sights you can get your hands on," Casanova said. "If at all possible, also try to find someone with competition-based iron sights. The typical irons that come with a lot of ARs are not a fair test of the system. Figure out what feels more natural for you and then stick with it. Take advantage of opportunities to talk with others who are more experienced with the same system you're using.

"Do your homework. Know whatever system you are running, what the sub-tensions of the different parts are at differ-

ent ranges, what your ballistics are," Casanova continued. "That kind of information will make you a lot more successful at all ranges. Try *everything*. Just because you're running one thing now doesn't necessarily mean something else won't work better. Work the fundamentals, too, like trigger control and cheek weld, which will help no matter what equipment you shoot. Test, test, *test,* and pay attention to what you see happening out on the range. Also, shoot as many matches, especially the bigger matches, as you can. There is no substitute for that experience."

Iron sight shooters, perhaps more than variable power scope users, understand the benefit of lots of rifle practice, especially in the awkward shooting positions from which stages will be shot. An iron sight shooter must know the ballistics of their bullets, where the impact will occur at every distance and, more importantly, what the sight picture should look like in order to break the shot.

"I focus mostly on knowing my sight picture at different ranges," said Casanova. "If I can hold the image in my head of the sight picture I need, then the position I am shooting a target from doesn't matter. I do practice positions, too, but not as much. A large part of the sight picture work I do includes working with my ballistics and knowing what a particular load is going to do in different conditions."

The reason for so much rifle practice is the target presentation itself. Iron sight shooters have long bemoaned the fact that long-range rifle targets at Outlaw 3-gun events almost exclusively put the platform at a disadvantage. The lack of contrasting backgrounds, changing light conditions in sun and shade, and the size of steel targets at distances ranging from 200 to 550 yards combine to make iron sight rife shooting an extremely tough endeavor.

"FNH was the best match for Tactical Iron last year," Vaught said. "Ozarks had the targets in plain view, but they were little and skinny. The only thing I don't like to see are stages where there is a great deal of variability in target presentation during different times of day."

Natural terrain matches are quite often the biggest offender, regarding long-range rifle target placement, with hills, trees, and valleys casting a wide range of sun and shade conditions, not to mention foliage and the hues present in forest or desert landscapes. Take an unpainted piece of gray steel, drop it in one of these backgrounds, and it seems to melt away. Too, a 100-yard range bay can be just as challenging when the sun sets behind the berm, placing the targets in darkness while shining the last available light directly into the competitors' eyes.

But, at the end of the day, for most Tactical Iron shooters, there's still value in shooting what was once a seemingly dwindling division. The challenge of ringing steel *without* using the latest and greatest in optics is a major draw to most of the die-hard Tactical Iron shooters.

"Matches need to keep Tactical Iron, because it offers those guys with a basic AR or patrol-type rifle with a dot a division to shoot in and not be under-gunned," Vaught said. "Plus, there are guys like me who just really get a bigger kick out of the basic principles of rifle-craft than they

do getting into a technology race.

"Shooters should consider the TI division, because it's easy to get equipment for and be competitive," Vaught continued. "It takes and builds on strong, fundamental shooting skills. Your rifle will not be burdened by one of those ugly tube-like things bolted to the top of it. Other

(top) Brian Vaught engages rifle targets on his way to becoming the 2011 Kentucky State Champion in Tactical Iron at the Kentucky Stage Multi-Gun Championships. Above, he runs his Tactical Iron rifle during, the 2011 ARFCOM-Rockcastle Pro-Am.

shooters will think it was luck, when you hit your first 300-yard flasher with irons—until you hit the next 10."

More importantly, the Tactical Iron rifle is the one many new shooters are most likely to own. Therefore, Tactical Iron remains an equipment division essential to the effort of keeping the sport of 3-gun accessible to the widest range of potential shooters.

"I shot a local match last month here in Kentucky," Vaught said. "Of 57 shooters, the largest division was TI. I think it could get deeper."

The Tactical Iron division most likely *wouldn't* be considered deep at most major 3-gun matches, despite the allowance of 1X optics. Nevertheless, the race for the 2011 3GN Tactical Iron Division Championship was an exciting one—a sprint to the final wire between Kurt Miller, Kelly Neal, and James Casanova.

With two matches left in the season, Casanova failed in his bid to pick up a pivotal second overall win for the season, effectively eliminating him from the title—yet, he would still have a say in who would win. At the final points match of the season, the FNH USA 3-Gun Championship, Casanova knocked off Kelly Neal, thereby giving the title to the division veteran and iron sight shooter Kurt Miller, who edged Casanova by a mere .63 for the season in the final standings and a score that was nearly 14 points ahead of Neal.

After all the hype, controversy, and debate surrounding the inclusion of 1X optics, the division still belonged to the iron sight shooters, though the availability of 1X optics had unleashed an infusion of new blood into the ranks.

"Limited division is really cool and the foundation of the game, at least as far as equipment goes," Kelley said. "It is the home of a diehard group that has mastered the fundamentals of marksmanship and firmly believes that, if they can see it, they'll hit it. It employs good, basic gear that is relatively inexpensive and easy to maintain. Still, until the inclusion of 1X optics, I would have said it was not a place for the new guy to get started. Iron-sighted rifles take more time and effort to learn to use well, and that learning curve can discourage the newbie from playing. But, bolt on a 1X optic, and the new guy gets better faster—and, as a 3-gunner, better and faster is where we all want to be!"

Heavy Metal

Diligentia, Vis, Celeritas.
Accuracy, Power, Speed.

This is the principle upon which practical shooting—combat shooting—was founded.

"Speed without accuracy is useless, as is accuracy without speed, and both together may not suffice without power."—*Marine Colonel Jeff Cooper, the Father of Practical Shooting*

By early in the 2000s, yet another sub-movement was beginning to take shape in the ever evolving world of 3-gun. In some ways, it mirrored the same type of thinking that had led to the first SOF match so many years before. This time, a growing number of shooters saw the need for a special division within 3-gun competitions, one that rewarded the use of true, combat-proven gun and cartridge platforms.

Much of the debate about

modern handguns and rifles in America has centered around one topic—power. In hunting circles, the debate took the form of .270 versus .30-06 and O'Connor versus Keith. In combat shooting, the argument matured into major versus minor power factor, or the formula derived to measure the momentum of a fired projectile (mass x velocity/1,000 = power factor). In basic terms, minor caliber in 3-gun competition most often represents the modern NATO chambering currently deployed by most nations—9mm double-stack pistols and .223-based AR-style rifles. Major power factor comes from the military guns of yesteryear, most often viewed through "Old Slabsides," the Government Model 1911 in .45 ACP, along with the M14 (or Springfield M1As, in civilian circles), and its .308 chambering. While IPSC pistol or Bianchi Cup use the definition of power factor to achieve benchmarks in a slightly different way, in Outlaw 3-gun, power factor really only applies to Heavy Metal, meaning it's either Heavy or it isn't.

This debate has raged on from the time the U.S. military switched from the fabled M14, that wonderful battle rifle fashioned from wood and steel, to the much maligned, at least in its early years, M16 platform. In the 1980s, the iconic M1911 was replaced by the Beretta 92F, with the 9mm pushing the venerable .45 out of military use. "Power"

was indeed one of the founding principles behind combat shooting itself, as well as the original dogma upon which IPSC shooting was born. As such, as specialized race guns took over the winners podiums in practical shooting, it became only a matter of time before a strong push for a return of these founding principles returned. In 3-gun, that movement was realized in the form of the He-Man, or Heavy Metal, division.

"To the best of my knowledge, Pueblo, New Mexico, Police Department Captain Eddie Rhodes* coined the name 'He-Man,'" said Patrick Kelley, who is probably the most accomplished Heavy Metal 3-Gun competitor in the division's nearly decade-long

history. "He also proposed the equipment guidelines that called for a return to our founding principles. Rhodes' idea was to generate healthy competition by using full-power, heavy-caliber ammunition delivered from basic patrol car or home-defense gear. So, He-Man is a revisit to our combat roots and is *not* a retro or antique division. We have divisions for the low-recoil, go-fast guns. And, thanks to Captain Rhodes, we now have one for the power tools of the game."

"I came up with a concept that we now call He-Man," Eddie Rhodes said in an interview at the 2008 DPMS Tri-Gun. "It involved using a .308 rifle at a power factor of military ball, a .45-caliber handgun with a power factor of military ball, and a 12-gauge shotgun shooting buckshot and slugs only. We called it He-Man, and some other matches have called it Heavy Metal."

On the outside, Heavy Metal might seem like a difficult division in which to get started. In reality, for some shooters, the cost is likely to be much less than that it will take to assemble the more specialized gear seen in larger equipment divisions. The beauty of Heavy Metal, to many, is that the gear is indeed Spartan. A pump shotgun, a .45 pistol, and a .308 rifle will get you onto the playing field.

"The initial cost is less expensive than that of likely any other division," competitor Bryan Ray said. "A pump shotgun set up for 3-gun will cost less than half

Tate Moots takes on long-range rifle targets with his Heavy Metal Optics division rifle, during the 2011 Rocky Mountain 3-Gun.

that of a good semi-automatic. Almost everyone has a .45 ACP that can be used, but, if not, a Glock or Springfield XD in .45 can be bought for under $600. The rifle isn't much more expensive than any iron-sighted AR set up for 3-gun, whether the competitor chooses an M1A, one of the various .308 ARs, or even an FAL. The money saved by not having to buy an optic can go toward a lot of ammo. Guns using .308 ammo run roughly twice the cost of .223, but, if the competitor keeps this in mind, it makes a good sight picture just a little more important! I shoot almost all local matches in Tac Irons with a .223 AR and a 9mm or .40-caliber pistol so that I can save the expensive ammo for major matches."

Indeed, in a gear-driven sport, Heavy Metal (and, to be fair, Tactical Iron, as well), serves as the inclusive and accessible division for 3-gun. Gun guys and gals are creatures of habit, and so many of them who already have a .45 pistol are just as likely to have a pump gun and a surplus-type .308 in the safe. Or they may need only one of the trio to have what's needed to jump into their first match. This commonality, combined with some shooters' interest in military history and martial arms, makes Heavy Metal an obvious place for some to get started in 3-gun.

"My late father-in-law was drafted into the Army, in 1967, and was trained on the M14 in basic," Ray said. "After hearing him talk about how much he enjoyed the M14, I bought a Springfield M1A, around 1998, with intentions of shooting High Power matches. That never happened, so the rifle sat in my safe until 2008, when I signed up for

my first 3-gun match, the Blue Ridge Mountain 3-Gun. I studied the divisions to see what I could shoot without buying a bunch of extra gear. There was a Remington 870 Police in my closet, a single-stack 1911 I used in USPSA, and the M1A. I shot my first match with this gear, running out of shotgun shells on almost every stage, stuffing rifle magazines into my back pockets, and had the time of my life. I came in second at this match behind the late, great Eddie Rhodes and was hooked on Heavy Metal."

Heavy Metal, though often

the smallest division at many major matches, soon developed a small but loyal following, with competitors such as the late Eddie Rhodes, Patrick Kelley, and others putting big-bore action shooting on display. This is the division of loud, hard-kicking rifles and pistols, as well as the pump-action shotgun. The calibers are bigger, the recoil more pronounced, and the strategy—and most always the hardships—completely different than in any other 3-gun division.

"Heavy Metal is not for everyone," Kelley said. "You have

to be willing to put more effort into training than most any other division. The reason for this is torque and recoil. No matter the platform or the modifications, .308s produce more torque and recoil for the competitor to deal with than .223s. Same goes for the fixed-breech 12-gauge pump-action shotgun versus the recoil-mitigating auto-loader. Ammo management with these guns is a hurdle to jump, too.

Competing in Heavy Metal Optics, Jansen Jones conducts a magazine change, during a stage at the 2011 Rocky Mountain 3-Gun.

Remember, you, as a Heavy Metalist, have only 20 rounds per .308 magazine versus 30, 40, or more for the .223 shooter. This applies to your handgun, too, where you have just eight to 10 rounds in your .45 ACP of choice versus 20-plus rounds of .40 S&W or 9mm. I'm not selling this very well, am I?"

"This gear is *heavy*!" said Bryan Ray, who, at 165 pounds, has emerged as one of the country's top Heavy Metal competitors over the last couple seasons. "Between a 12-pound rifle, steel magazines, and the ammo, it's a *lot* to carry from start to finish on a stage. Shot-to-shot time with the rifle is a little slower due to the recoil, and, when targets must be engaged from some sort of wobbly prop (like the boat and dock at Ozark and reacquisition of the sights a little more difficult. Contorted positions while running the pump shotgun can get almost to the painful category. At Benning, in 2010, I remember shooting from within the Cooper tunnel, and while I'm working on the right-hand targets, it crossed my mind that I had never once practiced operating the pump shotgun support side, let alone while doubled up inside a tunnel. I still don't practice it, but now I at least know what to expect."

Despite the pain, Heavy Metal offers a place to play for those competitors who enjoy loud, big-banging guns. Nowhere is that more apparent than in the selection of Heavy Metal rifles, where modern-day renditions of World War II and Korea infantry guns still reign supreme, alongside specialized AR-10 variants and piston-driven rifles made for modern war fighters.

"Heavy Metal, unlike all the

other divisions is *not* ruled by the AR-15 platform," Kelley said. Major 3-gun events have been won with FALs, AR-10s, and the M1A rifles, placing additional truth on the adage 'It is the Indian, not the arrow.' For me, Springfield Armory's National Match M1A feels like it was born for this division. Accurate and completely reliable out of the box, sporting a 22-inch medium-weight barrel, match trigger, and excellent sights, expertly assembled and glass bedded to an oversized walnut stock, this rifle rocks! You might find more accuracy within the AR platform, but the M1A was built as a .308 from the ground up and was the original box-fed U.S. battle tested 'war club.' It lives up to this moniker very well indeed.

"Of the AR platforms, Armalite, DPMS, and POF-USA all make .308 rifles that are fully suitable as manufactured," Kelley continued. "Many competitors, when making the switch to Heavy Metal, are just supersizing their 'mouse' guns, giving them a potential leg up on those cross training to a different platform. As mentioned before, FALs win matches, too, and it's no wonder. The FAL has proven itself in harm's way all over the world and is the most prolific self-loading .308 military rifle in history. If you just want the best, the crew at DSA would be happy to outfit you, offering several models suitable for the Heavy Metal enthusiast. For the more budget conscience, one could get under way with less initial expenditure if you are willing to undertake a do-it-yourself project by assembling your FAL from surplus parts."

Today, more rifle manufacturers than ever before produce

.308-based AR-style rifles, giving 3-gun competitors tremendous options in that market. And new offerings, such as the SCAR 17, are just now being explored in competition. Better still, competitors no longer have to rely on surplus ammunition, as nearly every major ammunition manufacturer produces one or more match-grade .308 variant suitable for 3-gun.

"When I started competing, South African military surplus .308 is what I used, because it was available," Ray said. "As my supply ran out, I switched to Federal American Eagle 150-grain .308. It provides adequate accuracy through my rifle, with 100-percent reliability, and it's affordable for major matches at about $.55 per round. Most of the 168-grain loads are a little more accurate, but, with iron sights, I can't tell the difference between 1 MOA (minute of angle) and 2 MOA during the stress of a stage.

"My rifle is zeroed at 200 yards, because the trajectory is virtually flat from muzzle to 200 using this zero. I adjust the point of impact for elevation based on the stage either before the buzzer or after, depending on target distances. I prefer the same sight picture on every target, so I will dial elevation during a course of fire, if necessary. (I do hold for wind, though, rather than adjust the sight.) If there is a target at 225 yards and another at 275, I'll dial for 250 and shoot both with this setting, as the point of impact is close enough at both distances for a scored hit on an MGM flasher."

Jeff Cooper's Modern Technique, Gunsite, IPSC—nearly everything we associate with combat or practical shooting be-

gan with a single-stack .45-caliber pistol. As such, Heavy Metal is the only place a 1911-style pistol can still call home and remain competitive in 3-gun. However, the division is not limited to the original warhorse. Glocks, Springfield XDs, Smith & Wesson M&Ps, and more can all play in Heavy Metal, with ammunition capacity being the only real restriction regarding which models make the cut. It's that magazine capacity, generally eight rounds in a 1911 or 10 in a double-stacked pistol that becomes the game-changer for every competitor in Heavy Metal.

"When selecting a pistol, the

Heavy Metal division is *the* home for the single-stack 1911 in .45 ACP," Kelley said. "With either eight-round flush-fit or slightly extended 10-round magazines, this old yet ever-new combat- and competition-perfected pistol dovetails nicely into the fray. But, as much as I love that classic machine, when the event calls for 10 rounds on board, you'll generally find a Glock G21 in my holster. My reasons are twofold. First, all have passive safeties. Courses of fire require 'safety on' or 'gun empty' abandonment for the transition to long gun. Under the stress of time management, and with an immediate

Patrick Kelley is one of the most dominant Heavy Metal shooter in the history of the sport's division.

disqualification from the match for a violation of this rule, passive safeties are 'automatic.' Pick your flavor here—Glock, Springfield, or Smith & Wesson all play the game very well. Second, call it fashion sense, but extended 10-round .45 ACP mags and the 1911 just clash."

The limited round availability also creates a clash in stage design, as most match directors cater their stage plans around magazine capacities exceeding 20 rounds, meaning Heavy Metal

shooters are subjected to twice as many magazine changes on high-volume pistol stages. To compete at a high level, the pistol game in Heavy Metal becomes more about accuracy and ammo management than the full-out speed seen in the Tactical Optics or Open divisions.

"You have only 10 rounds in the magazine, make each shot count," Bryan Ray said. "With the trend in 3-gun heading toward reactive pistol targets, it's easy to waste a lot of time reloading, if the shooter isn't getting hits. Practice doesn't have to be on an expensive plate rack, the head of a USPSA target works great, also."

The third level of Heavy Metal punishment comes in the form of the shotgun. While every other division in 3-gun allows an autoloader, Heavy Metal shooters are restricted to the pump-action. Still, the nearly universal choice for law enforcement, military, and even home-defense, the pump gun, then, could be considered the most "practical" of all the platforms currently used in the sport. Still, the pump gun is an interesting enigma. It is the most basic of all firearms used in this game, yet the pump gun is poorly understood and much maligned by many who don't use one. But make no mistake, in the right hands, a pump gun is a remarkable firearm on display. For the rest of us, running a pump can be considered the lost art of practical shooting.

"Sometimes I think the art is lost on me!" Bryan Ray said. "Just when a competitor feels real comfortable with the pump gun, they'll short-stroke it at the worst possible moment. I don't know how many times I've done that with an aerial clay at

12 o'clock. It's not much slower to operate a pump gun than an auto, if the targets can be shot from a standing position, but throw in a barricade to shoot around or under, and it can become challenging."

Compared to the complex, specialized race guns elsewhere in the sport, the pump-action shotgun is likely the most simple tool of the trade. Yet, for those outside the division, it might also be the least understood.

"When it comes to 3-gunning, shooters generally overlook the pump shotgun as a competition tool, and I understand why," Kelley said. "First, the poor pump lacks the important 'gee-whiz' factor the self-loaders have. And, for some of the 'cool kids,' it's better to look good than to shoot well. When you do see them, they are in the hands of the new guy—or in the experienced hands of the 'old dude.' Do yourself a favor here and watch out for that old dude, it might be me!

"Second, the pump is only as reliable as the person operating it, making the shooter a critical component. No matter the Internet bull, in human hands they don't cycle faster than an auto. To do that would mean cycling faster than 0.12 seconds between shots, and that is 500 rounds per minute, kids. That ain't happening!

"Third, the act of pumping is made even more difficult from awkward positions, and, fourth, the pump-gun transmits more recoil to you than does an auto! But, laying down a wicked-fast run that's met with a few hoots of approval is even cooler when the hooters never even *noticed* you were shooting a pump. Running a pump-gun at that speed is a unique experience and well worth the effort. That alone is reason enough to play. Heavy Metal, baby! Yea!"

It should also be considered that the mechanism that makes a pump gun, the physical act of running the fore-end through its entire range of motion, is a simple, yet overlooked, part of pump-gunning under the stress of match conditions. Inaccurate shooting, shooter-induced malfunctions, and unintentionally running the gun dry are common mistakes made by Heavy Metal pump-gunners—inexperienced and veterans alike.

"It's easy to miss a target, if you're thinking about operating the bolt while squeezing the trigger," Ray said. "Similarly, when the bolt slams back into battery, the muzzle tends to dip a little. If you're too quick on the trigger here, the shots tend to be low. It's a little easier to miss a target with a pump gun than an auto, if the shooter doesn't take these things into account. Also, if the shooter loses count on the load, he usually doesn't realize the gun is empty until it goes "click," since the bolt will go forward on an empty chamber."

In Heavy Metal, the rifle is heavy and loud, it kicks harder, and the ammo itself is more expensive. The pistol, too, packs more punch, .45 costs more than 9mm, and the limited capacity makes stage breakdowns even more challenging. Finally, the shotgun is much more of a thumper; without the recoil-mitigating process imparted by the autoloader, the Heavy Metal shooter is subjected to extra foot-pounds of 12-gauge energy. These three gun types, taken each to their own in the context of Heavy Metal shooting, drastically changes the game. However, it's the full sum of its parts that paints the entire picture of what it means to play in this division. Heavy Metal is the land where big boys play, and where the meek are found wanting.

"As I stated before, Heavy Metal is not a retro or antique division," Kelley said. "It's a place that offers great personal reward for excellence in overcoming equipment challenges not faced in other divisions. It's a place closer to the roots of Practical Shooting. It's a place where you meet the challenge head-on with the tools, rather than adjusting the tools to meet the challenge, and it's a place where accuracy, power, and speed are points of pride. The Heavy Metalist must be consistently accurate, as capacity is limited. Power—and we generate much—is intrinsic to our weapons. To effectively demonstrate speed within this division means you have mastered technique."

"It's just another challenge within the world of 3-gun," Ray said. "The stages are the same as the ones all the other competitors shoot, but they have to be looked at a little differently, considering the capacity restrictions on the rifle and pistol—but, then again, it also gives the shooter a little personal satisfaction, when the range staff has to repair rifle targets after a .308 breaks them!"

As such, Heavy Metal caters to the 3-gunner who is a breed apart. To understand that is to realize we're talking about a niche within a niche, a sub-segment within a sub-segment. While 3-gun may be the fastest growing of all the shooting sports, within that body of shooters is a smaller, crazier, band of colorful characters who enjoy pain and relish thumping steel targets with a hammer bigger than anyone else's.

"I think Heavy is the division guys shoot because they sincerely enjoy the equipment they're using," Ray sad. "Some people compete in Open because they like to go fast, or in Tac Optics because they like to shoot against the most competitors, but most of the shooters in HM choose the division because they just want to shoot a big, loud rifle and a .45. It's sort of the cowboy division of 3-gun."

Today, Heavy Metal is actually two divisions, thanks to the addition of Heavy Metal Optics some years ago—a point of contention at some matches and one celebrated at others. As such, Heavy Metal Optics has perhaps the widest-ranging set of rules defining the approved equipment list for the division, including variances in pistol caliber and, amazingly,

Rob Romero, normally a Tactical Optics competitor, jumped to Heavy Metal, in late 2011, to make a run at the 3GN Heavy Metal Division Championship—which he won by taking the final three matches of the season.

even shotgun type—pump guns at some matches, autoloaders at others. With the addition of 1X optics now allowed at some venues for traditional limited divisions such as Heavy Metal, the varying sets of rules that govern the sport become ever more complicated. Some have argued that Heavy Metal and Heavy Metal Optics should be re-combined on the national stage, which would, in theory, make one stronger division having a higher level of competition for all.

As it stands, and though Heavy in both its forms may be small, there are still plenty of mighty shooters who regularly shoot the divisions. Patrick Kelley has long dominated in Heavy Metal, and Rob Romero jumped into the mix, in 2010, to win the inaugural 3GN Heavy Metal Division Championship. Bryan Ray, in just a couple of years of shooting major 3-gun events, won two division titles last season and has become a real threat in Heavy Metal.

In Heavy Metal Optics, Barry Dueck and Adam Popplewell were a cut above the field in 2010, waging a season-long battle for the 3GN Heavy Metal Optics Division Championship that Barry Dueck won during the season's final weekend. Jansen Jones, Mark Hanish, and a host of other solid shooters also regularly play in Heavy Metal Optics.

"There are some terrific shooters in Heavy Metal right now," Rhodes said, in 2008. "Yeah, it's kind of a rough road to hoe anymore. You have the good shooters, and then you have the equipment that kind of beats you up a little more than that in some of the other divisions."

In August 2012, Heavy Metal will receive another shot in the arm, with the debut of a new major match—the He-Man 3-Gun Championship, otherwise known within the 3-gun community as the "Big Johnson." The Big Johnson moniker is apt, a tribute to JJ and Denise Johnson, the Rocky Mountain 3-Gun match directors who remain vocal supporters of keeping rules in place that encourage participation in the smaller divisions, rather than limit them. To their credit, they are fierce protectors of everything "He-Man," the term originally coined by Captain Rhodes to describe the military ball division of a bygone American era—and maybe one that shouldn't be so bygone after all.

I don't believe just anyone could successfully put on a Heavy Metal-only match. However, the Johnsons are undoubtedly the most well suited of all the major Outlaw match directors to design and run such an event. First, and most importantly, JJ Johnson is a top Heavy Metal competitor, finishing fourth in the nation in the 3GN Heavy Metal Division. But, he and Denise are also intimately familiar with the venue, the NRA's amazing Whittington Center, in Raton, New Mexico. So, now a guy who knows the ins and outs of .308 competition has a match dedicated to the platform and 30,000 acres on which to test his ability to run it. The mix should provide for some absolutely wicked long-range rifle stages, a staple of the Rocky Mountain matches for many years.

Bryan Ray exploded onto the top ranks of the Heavy Metal division, in 2011. Here he loads his Benelli Nova during a stage at the 2011 AR15.Com-Rockcastle Pro-Am.

If successful, the He-Man 3-Gun Championship will become the most challenging test in the sport for how competitors handle power. In a real way, the crew who runs Rocky Mountain, the legacy of the original Soldier of Fortune match, is taking the sport of 3-gun back to its roots;

at SOF, in 1980, the winners used M1As, H&K 91s, and single-stack 1911s—some of which will surely be in plain sight in Raton for years to come.

"Dust off that pump gun and load-up that single stack," Patrick Kelley said. "Get your hands on a fine, self-loading .308 and join Club Torque and Recoil. I can tell you firsthand that victory is a little sweeter for the Heavy Metalist."

*The sport of 3-gun suffered a terrible tragedy, March 15, 2010, when, during a training run, Captain Eddie Rhodes, the father of the "He-Man" division, suffered a heart attack and passed away. Those in the 3-gun world who knew him best honor his memory—none more so than the staff and crew at Rocky Mountain and their new He-Man 3-Gun Championship.

"He was a fierce competitor, a warrior, and a man among men," said Patrick Kelley. "Those who shared the range with him are better for the experience. I know I am."

Wide-Open Shotgunning:
XRAIL vs. Saiga

The Russian Bear

Over the last few 3-gun seasons, no single gun design has changed an individual division more than the Saiga shotgun has the Open. What once took several seconds to load—whatever time it took a competitor to go to the speedloader multiple times—could now be achieved in a fraction of the time with a simple magazine change. While the Saiga 12 has been manufactured in Russia since the 1990s (it was previously imported by EAA, and now through Russian American Armory), it took a little American ingenuity to bring the Saiga to the point where it's made an impact.

For a multitude of reasons, the Saiga simply wasn't reliable enough to stand up to the demands of 3-gun competition. But seeing the potential in a box magazine-fed shotgun system, several gunsmiths went to work perfecting the system. One of the most successful of that group has been Robert Wright and his R&R Racing out of Oregon.

When one hears of the laborious process it takes to get a Saiga running reliably, you have to wonder why on earth a gunsmith would want to take on such a task. For Wright, it all started as a project of necessity, but one that's paid huge dividends in the long run.

"I switch divisions every two years and needed a mag-fed shotgun for Open division," Wright explained. "I knew that a mag-fed gun was the only way to go, and my plan was to buy a gun and the parts to build a gun. But nobody made any parts that were any good, so I started making the parts.

"One day, I was on the phone talking to my friend Paul from MSTN and told him about my gun project. He talked me into building him a gun—and then another. Things started taking off from there, and now I'm working on an FBI contract. I beat out several companies to come up with a breaching gun."

Wright takes imported Saigas and completely overhauls the entire shotgun, hogging out material and machining many new parts—a multitude of processes are required to get the imported shotgun competition ready.

"It is easier to tell you what I *don't* do," Wright said. "I do seven processes on the barrel alone. The receiver gets about 15, while the carrier gets five. The dust cover gets three, and the bolt gets three. I bet that I go through more than 60 processes on each gun, and every gun is built the way I build my own. I will not cut any corner to save time or money. When you buy one of my guns, it is first-cabin all the way.

"I shorten the gas system so the gun will have enough gas to run the comp," Wright continued. "I also build my own pistons, op rods, op rod tubes, and gas plugs. The guns still say Saiga on the side, only because the ATF makes me leave it. But they are as far from a Saiga as you can get. The guns as they come to me are very crude and inconsistent, and that's why you see so many that don't work. Most people just move the trigger forward and add a stock."

Expensive and time consuming, Wright's overhauls turn a lumbering, Spartan import into a smooth, versatile machine. The proof, for Wright, is all measured in time—the name of the game in 3-gun.

"When I used to shoot Tactical, I could load a shell in a second from shot-to-shot," Wright said. "That was on a really good day, when the stars were aligned just right. Now I can load 12 rounds in under 1½ seconds. I shoot my gun like I shoot a Limited 10 pistol—when in doubt, put in a fresh mag. With a tube gun, you can't afford to miss a shot, because it will cost

you a second for a make-up shot. But, with a box mag, going from birdshot to slugs to buck is just a mag change. And you can stack rounds in the mag to go from bird to buck or slugs. Because all the rounds are so close to the shooter, the box mag guns transition faster than a tube gun. In fact, my guns transition even faster than a tube gun with an XRAIL. Plus, when you pick up one of my guns, it feels like your AR rifle, so you don't have to think as much."

For shooters new to 3-gun, the Saiga represents an easier first step into the game, as one isn't required to learn the weak- or strong-hand reloading techniques employed in other divisions—not an overly complicated chore, but a time consuming one. The Saiga delivers a sys-

tem readily familiar to most any shooter who can execute a magazine change.

Nowhere is that impact potential more apparent than in the 3-gun career of Clint Upchurch, a solid USPSA pistol shooter who jumped into 3-gun two years ago and right into the Open division.

"I felt that reloading the Saiga was *so* much faster," Upchurch said. "And the flexibility of magazine configurations allowed options that made the Saiga easier to manage than the other platforms. The controls of the R&R Saiga were very user friendly. I liked the left-side charg-

The Saiga had the big advantage of being one of the fastest reloadable guns ever made, but it's overall quality wasn't up to the rigors of 3-gun competition. Robin Wright has been one of just a few successful gunsmiths to overhaul this gun into the one every 3-gunner dreams of shooting.

ing handle, and the safeties and mag release were just like those on an AR-15. To me, it seemed easier to operate than a traditional tube-fed shotgun. It was definitely easier to learn the platform—mainly because of the AR-15 similarities."

Upchurch, after only two years in the sport, exploded onto the national 3-gun scene by winning six major matches and outlasting a late-season push from both Jerry Miculek and Mike Voigt to win the 2011 3-Gun Nation Open Division Championship. While Upchurch clearly has tremendous game in all areas of 3-gunning, he nevertheless acknowledges an advantage provided by his R&R Saiga.

"The Saiga proved to be advantageous on a many occasions," Upchurch said. "Anytime we shot the big field courses with lots of shotgun targets I had an advantage. On the quick, low-round count stages, the shotguns were pretty much equal."

The X-Factor

RCI's Mark Roth is "constant"—constant movement, constant talking, constant smoking—a man of perpetual motion and ideas. So when the 3-gun bug bit Roth several years ago, I suspect his mind and actions were constantly revolving around every aspect of the sport.

That's an over-simplified portrait of my friend, for sure, but it helps set up what happens next. A contractor by trade, one who had built a successful business in his Appleton, Wisconsin, home, Roth was talking with DPMS' Bruce Piatt, while their squad waited to shoot a stage at the 2006 DPMS Tri-Gun. As the conversation progressed, the two began discussing the idea of adding more capacity to a tubular magazine shotgun without extending the tube beyond manageable lengths.

Once turned onto the subject, I'm sure it was only a matter of time before Mark's mind found a solution for the problem. A few weeks later, Mark's thoughts become the XRAIL.

For those not in the know, the XRAIL (Xtreme Roth Auto Indexing Loader) is a self-articulating, high-capacity, magazine-tube extension for tubular magazine shotguns. Consisting of multiple auxiliary tubes, once all the shotshells in the first tube have been emptied, the XRAIL

automatically indexes the next auxiliary tube into place to feed the main tube. And, because it's self-indexing, one can load it full and shoot it dry without making any adjustments. Incredibly, the system increases magazine capacity up to 23 rounds, depending on the shotgun platform.

"The XRAIL consists of four magazine tubes that work off a central axis—one primary tube and three auxiliary tubes," Roth said. "The system is added to the end of the existing shotgun magazine tube in the same fashion as a traditional magazine tube extension. It does not change the function of your gun."

Once installed, shotshells are loaded into the gun in a traditional manner, right through the existing loading port on the shotgun.

"To load, simply load the primary tube full and manually rotate the tube housing to access the first auxiliary tube," Roth said. "Load the first auxiliary tube and rotate to the second tube. Repeat the process until all the tubes are loaded. When firing, once a tube is emptied, the system rotates to the next tube and so forth, until the gun is empty. The primary tube is the first tube loaded and the last one emptied, and it is also the only tube with a spring and follower that extends down into the receiver of the gun."

In competition, the interesting component of the XRAIL involves sequencing on stages that mix two different loads within that stage—most often birdshot and slugs. In whatever order the targets are engaged, the loading sequence must be reversed in order to come out correctly. For example, during a particular shotgun stage at Ozark, in 2010, FN's Tommy Thacker, who was running an XRAIL on his SLP, faced a stage mixed with 16 birdshot targets and four that required slugs.

"The way I set it up," explained Thacker, "is that I look at how I'm going to shoot the course of fire, and I lay my shells out exactly that way. Then I have to load them backwards, so that the round I want to shoot last has to go into the gun first."

Along with Roth himself, XRAIL as a company has begun to build a stable of quality shooters who are running the accessory in competition, including Nick Kalishek, Tony Holmes, Jerry Miculek, and

2012 3GN Champion Tommy Thacker.

"Since the introduction of our product, we have been fortunate to have the world's greatest shooters want use our product," Roth said. "We are very happy to see that our vision has been realized by others of such distinction. We are seeing that the great shooters such as Larry Houck, Tommy Thacker, and Tony Holmes are excited to use our product, because of the advantages they gain on a gun they trust. Having shooters of this caliber trust and use our product is equivalent to having Tiger Woods use your golf clubs."

XRAIL units are currently available for Remington models 870, 1187, 1100, and Versa Max; Benelli Super Black Eagle, Super Black Eagle 2, and the M1, M2, and M2 Tactical; FNH USA SLP; Mossberg 930; and the Winchester Super X3 shotguns. Retail is around $700 for a full-sized unit, $650 for a compact model.

XRAIL inventor Mark Roth of RCI, demos the XRAIL during the 2010 Superstition Mountain Mystery 3-Gun.

CHAPTER 6

THE FLIES

At many major 3-gun matches, the rifle becomes the difference maker, with long-range stages often becoming the one course of fire that separates the top shooters. However, rifle shooting certainly isn't *limited* to long-range targets in this sport. The rifle game is two or three games within the game, depending on your perspective.

It starts with close-range rifle targets. It might seem as though a target a mere few yards in front of the shooter would be simple, and, in truth, it is. It nevertheless requires some thought and preparation, and a working knowledge of mechanical offset and the rifle bullet's ballistics.

Most top 3-gunners, when using a scope in the optics divisions, run a rifle zeroed out to 200 yards, although there are certainly several using a 100-yard zero. Because an optic sits roughly 2.5 inches above the bore, and because the bullet trajectory has yet to climb to apex, the bullet will always impact low at close range.

At most any 3-gun match, stage designs will feature close-range paper targets set from a few feet out to 25 yards or so. To test a shooter's knowledge of mechanical offset and their focus to remember their holds under pressure, reduced-sized targets, or only the smaller "A" zone on an IPSC-type silhouette will be presented, giving a target area roughly the same size as a softball, at times. When the rifle is held center mass on this area, the bullet will likely impact low and out of the scoring area, due to mechanical offset. Knowing this, competitors aim high, often holding on the very top of the target, which delivers solid scoring hits.

Conversely, long-range targets test the other end of the spectrum. Here, and again in reference to Tactical Optics, a good reticle becomes important—one with mil-dots, descending stadia lines, or other means of holds below the center crosshair.

Running a 200-yard zero with a typical 55-grain match bullet, at 300 yards, that bullet drops down into the neighborhood of eight inches low. At 500 yards, it will likely be more than 50 inches low, depending on the bullet and load.

To complicate matters further, match directors, the evil monsters that they are, stra-tegically place long-range rifle targets at random distances such as 385 yards or 533 yards, distances that don't necessarily match the points of hold common in today's advanced reticles. For the shooter, this means testing each subtending reference mark by shooting match loads at every distance possible and creating a mental picture of what different target sizes and presentation look like, so as to provide cues on where to hold the rifle and break the shot.

Today, the rifle game at major 3-gun events is one that tests the full ballistic range of a competitor's rifle and load, along with the competitor's ability to get hits at extreme close- and long-range distances and everywhere in-between. Let's take a look at some of the guns and upgrades that are making the grade and winning matches.

Stag Arms Model 3G Competition

In 2011, Stag Arms, following the formation of its first sponsored 3-gun team with 3GN Pro Series competitors Jesse Tischauser and Kalani Laker, debuted a rifle built specifically for the sport. Best of all, Stag listened to the feedback provided by its shooters throughout the development process. The result was a rifle that has garnered high praise from within and without the 3-gun community.

The 3G Competition features an 18-inch stainless steel barrel, rifle-length gas system and Stag's own 3Gun compensator to reduce muzzle rise. A Geissele Super 3-Gun trigger is a solid upgrade. A Magpul ACS buttstock improves upon the standard A2- or M4-type designs.

A Samson Evolution free-floating handguard, one of the

Stag Arms Kalani Laker shoulders the new Stag Arms 3G Competition, a rifle that made a tremendous impact when it debuted in 2011.

hottest selling fore-ends in 2011, provided a significant upgrade over M4-style handguards. Dueck Defense RTS offset sights are available as an option. Utilizing upgraded components commonly seen on custom builds or from high-end rifle makers has made the 3G Competition one of the most out-of-the-box-ready rifles on the market. While Stag Arms isn't the first company to market a rifle specifically for the 3-gun market, its first offering is nevertheless a solid example of a reasonably priced gun featuring a well thought-out collection of aftermarket accessories commonly used in the sport.

JP Rifles Lower Program

John Paul Gangl's JP Rifles is, without question, one of the original companies to throw its full support into 3-gun. Gangl, a veteran competitor of many disciplines and a solid 3-gunner in his own right, knows the game inside and out. So, it's no surprise that his company remains a leader in high-end rifles built specifically for the needs of the action-shooting competitor.

Browse the JP website or catalog and you'll find several different variants, all of which use some combination of parts from Gangl's own design, such as heat sinks, improved triggers, buffers, and more. You will certainly pay more for a JP rifle than you would buying a "Brand X" M4, but you'll also get so much more rifle.

Veterans of the game seem to drift toward JP rifles, and JP-sponsored shooters regularly win major matches across the country. I see JP as the company that provides rifles for the customer who already plays this game and knows exactly what they want in a 3-gun rifle.

Continuing on that theme, one of the coolest options JP offers is the Lower Program. Here, customers can send in their stripped lower receiver for a semi-custom re-build, ranging from a fire control kit up to a complete reconstruction. As such, the Lower Program provides a more economical method to obtaining one of the coveted rifles on the 3-gun circuit.

FNH USA SCAR 16s

Bolstered by the competitive success of Team FNH USA, the ample coverage in the 3-Gun Nation Shoot-Off, and most definitely because of the association with the rifle's early trials in the SOCOM community, the FNH SCAR enjoys a certain mystique. In terms of 3-gun competitors, the SCAR is slowly building a following, showing up in more rifle racks at major matches each 3-gun season.

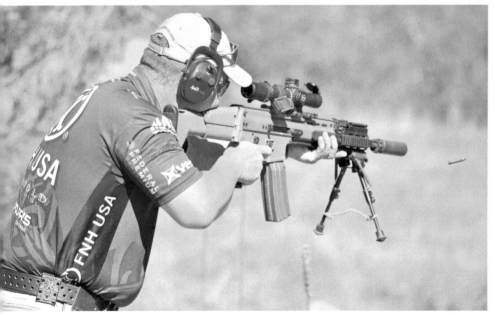

(above) Mark Hanish engages long-range rifle targets from a prone, supported position—as good a position as one is lucky enough to get in 3-gun—during the 2011 ARFCOM-Rockcastle Pro-Am.

(left) Open rifles are often tricked out with bipods, compensators/brakes and secondary optics.

Upchurch, Colt's CR Pro Competition landed the company squarely in the middle of what 3-gunners like in a competition gun. As such, Upchurch, along with FMG's Scott McGregor, has sung high praises for the gun.

With a Geissele trigger, 18-inch barrel, SureFire muzzle brake, and fully free-floated fore-end, the CR Pro utilizes many top accessories normally associated with custom builds. Similar to the Stag, yet made in much more limited numbers, the CR Pro really delivers quite a lot and stands out-of-the-box ready for high-level 3-gun competition. More than any of that, though, the Colt CR Pro may

Since Team FNH USA began competing heavily in 3-gun, the SCAR has steadily gained popularity among 3-gunners.

While most competitors still, and likely will for some time, prefer the AR-15 design for 3-gun, Team FNH USA shooters are effectively making an impression with the SCAR. Two 3GN Shoot-Off wins belong to FNH shooters, including 2011 and 2012 3GN Champion Tommy Thacker. Meanwhile, Dianna Liedorff is one of the top female competitors in the game, and the entire team is competitive in multiple equipment divisions.

In practical terms, the SCAR, while possessing operating controls, chambering, and a magazine system in the AR-sytle, has a different platform that requires getting used to. The piston-driven rifle recoils differently, the reciprocating bolt handle requires a new manual of arms, and the overall ergo-

nomics are a touch unique. But the SCAR shines in short-range rifle applications, especially working in and out of port windows, due to its compact design. At the same time, it delivers more than sufficient accuracy for long-range work.

Colt CR Pro Competition

Timed with the company's first sponsored shooter in 3GN Pro Series competitor Clint

Taran Butler runs a lightweight AR-15 and on short-range rifle targets is one of the fastest shooters in all of action shooting.

prove most seminal if history remembers the rifle, along with sponsorship of Upchurch, as one of many first steps in the long-awaited return of the company's prominence and significance in the civilian market.

The small collection of rifles listed here only begins to scratch the surface of what's available, as one could easily fill a book writing about semi-automatic rifles on the market today—even by limiting it to gear well suited to 3-gun. The rifle market has exploded, as has the popularity of 3-gun, and never a finer match of timing and opportunity has been in the world of rifles fit for practical shooting.

As good as are the many rifles available straight from the manufacturer, the most common rifle in 3-gun isn't made by any of them. Commonly referred to as a "Frankenstein," these are the AR-15 rifle builds carried out either by a gunsmith or the rifle owner himself. Indeed, many veteran shooters simply build their own rifle for 3-gun, outfitting it with exactly the right parts to fit very specific needs.

Lower Receivers

Stag Arms, DPMS, Del-Tone, Spike's Tactical—there are way too many to name—all manufacture and sell stripped lower receivers. They are available through a variety of sources such as Cheaper Than Dirt!, Midway USA, and Brownells. The Brownells website goes a step further, with its awesome AR Builder software that enables users to scroll through Brownells entire inventory and then "build" the perfect rifle. Either way, this is a low-cost way to get into a good 3-gun

rifle—for example, a laser-engraved Stag Arms stripped lower retails for around $150—and it's a great way to personalize your own rifle build while fitting the parts to suit your shooting needs.

Uppers

Depending on a shooter's needs, uppers are available in a wide range of variations, ranging from completely stripped uppers on the least expensive end, to fully specialized uppers with barrels, fore-ends, comps, and completely tricked out models from the likes of DPMS, JP Rifles, and more.

Piston rifles have seen an explosion in popularity over the last half decade, and inclusion in 3-gun competition has contributed to that interest. Adams Arms' Evolution Ultra Lite Upper features the popular Samson Manufacturing Evolution fore-end, a three-position adjustable gas block, and a .625-inch (muzzle diameter) Melonite-coated barrel. For those who lean more toward M4-type gear, Ruger offers a couple variations on 16-inch upper assemblies. Each upper utilizes Ruger's new two-stage piston design.

Brakes & Comps

No 3-gunner worth his salt would attempt to shoot a match without using a good muzzle brake or compensator. The name of this game is time, and a good comp keeps the muzzle rise down, which in turn gets the shooter back on target more quickly and ready to break the next shot.

DPMS manufactures the Jerry Miculek comp, a hold-over from the days when Miculek was a sponsored shooter for

One of the first upgrades many competitors make to their rifle is the addition of a better muzzle brake, like this one from SureFire.

(opposite) Though you don't see it a tremendous amount, the kneeling position is nevertheless a skill every 3-gunner should have, as demonstrated by SureFire's Maggie Reese.

DPMS, and it's a very popular choice among shooters. The Lund/SJC was designed by Team FNH USA shooter Erik Lund and S&J Custom and is another favorite with top competitors, as is Benny Hill's Rolling Thunder compensator.

SureFire Muzzle Brakes

SureFire muzzle brakes, which also happen to be attachment points for SureFire FastAttach Suppressors, have generated a lot of favor among competitors over the last few seasons. Sponsored shooters Barry Dueck (who heads the SureFire Suppressor Division) and Mike Voigt deigned the brakes, which utilize SureFire's proprietary Impulse Diffusion design, where minimal gas blowback is directed into the shooter's face.

"When we score these events, it's based on accuracy and speed," said Voigt. "One of the tools that I use to hit targets faster is the SureFire muzzle

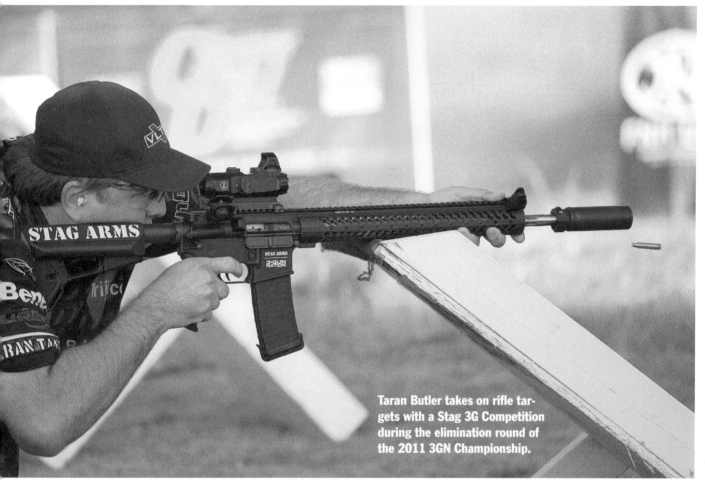

Taran Butler takes on rifle targets with a Stag 3G Competition during the elimination round of the 2011 3GN Championship.

brake. On an unsuppressed gun, you usually get a lot of movement up to the one to two o'clock area. When you put a muzzle brake on the gun, it reduces that rise. But, we've really tuned this brake to almost eliminate it."

"The bottom line with this is that, when I'm looking through the scope, I'm trying to acquire a target," Voigt said. "Once I fire, the target is right there again, it's waiting for me."

Stag Arms 3Gun Super Comp

Stag Arms, in conjunction with the launch of the new 3G Competition rifle, also developed a new compensator, the 3Gun Super Comp. I was the tackling of a new technology for the nimble AR manufacturer.

"It definitely wasn't easy," said Mark Malkowski, upon the release of the Super Comp. "We spent countless hours creating a muzzle device with the specific purpose of allowing a shooter to engage a second shot as quickly as their first."

The Super Comp utilizes cross drilling to vent gas upward, and a process called "nozzle technology" forms cones to propel the rifle back downward. At the same time, the weight balance allows gravity to counter muzzle rise.

Secondary Iron Sights

Ever since tactical and practical shooters began putting glass on rifles to serve as the primary sighting system, they began to search for better ways to back up the optics with iron

sights. In the tactical community, and in 3-gun events, flip-up iron sights became en

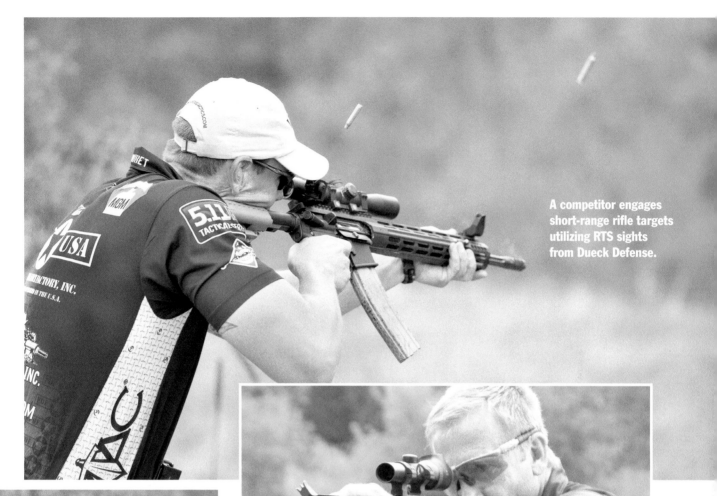

A competitor engages short-range rifle targets utilizing RTS sights from Dueck Defense.

Barry Dueck's RTS sights provide offset irons at a 45-degree angle from the main optic.

Open division shooter Mike Voigt hammers close-range rifle targets using a secondary rifle optic.

vogue—out of the way when you didn't need them, there in a flash when you did.

As Open shooters have known for some time, putting the secondary sighting system in a usable position is much more advantageous to the shooter. Today there are several different makes and models of sights hanging on seemingly every position in which one can be hung on an AR-15.

Dueck Defense RTS

Barry Dueck's Rapid Transition Sight (RTS) has become one of the more popular secondary iron sight systems in 3-gun. Dueck, a veteran of the Marine Corps and top 3-gun competitor, used his combined experience and took the old A2-stype sight from the M16 family, developed a mount to handle it at 45 degrees—just as Open shooters do with optics—and the RTS was born.

Because he used a military aperture and front sight post, the RTS is capable of accurate fire to surprisingly extended ranges. So, while the RTS is intended for use hosing closing-range targets, should the primary optic go down over any distance, shooters are still in the game with the RTS.

"A must-have for 3-gun shooting," said Practical Shooting Academy's Keith Garcia, a law enforcement officer and two-time 3-Gun Nation Shoot-Off winner. "The best back-up sight available anywhere. These sights are so sturdy I put a second set on my SWAT entry rifle."

Aftermarket Triggers

One of the first upgrades many shooters make to a stock rifle is an upgrade to the trigger system. JP Rifles, CMC, Geiselle, and AR Gold have all made good inroads in the sport, and their offerings come both as upgrade items on some rifles straight from the factory, or you can purchase them as aftermarket items. Brownells, Midway USA, and Cheaper Than Dirt! are all good sources for accessory trigger units. Depending on the model, some come as simple drop-in units, while others may need to be installed by a quality gunsmith.

Timney Triggers

One company making a push into 3-gun recently is Timney Triggers. Timney has built a solid reputation on its drop-in units that are a breeze to install. They drastically improve the trigger pull over a standard mil-spec trigger unit.

Modular in design, the completely "drop-in" unit from Timney is quickly gaining favor among 3-gunners.

For AR-15 designs, Timney's AR-15 Competition is pre-set to a pull weight ranging from three to five pounds. The Competition utilizes the rifle's original hammer and trigger pins. A true drop-in part, the Competition variant runs $210.

Due to the rising popularity of the FNH USA SCAR, Timney recently developed a SCAR variant built into an alloy housing and featuring a Teflon-nickel coating on the hammer. Also completely drop-in, the single-stage SCAR unit retails for around $310.

Ergo 2 Grip

One of the first parts 3-gunners often change out on a rifle is the grip. Top shooters swap out for better ergonomics, while other simply prefer different styles. Whatever the reason, Ergo Grips are one of the more popular aftermarket accessories in 3-gun.

The Ergo 2 SCAR Grip is designed specifically for the FNH USA SCAR, providing an over-molded, non-slip grip surface that improves upon the ergonomics of the standard grip. For AR-15 users, Ergo produces models in multiple styles and colors.

Grips are a common rifle upgrade by 3-gun competitors, such as this SCAR grip from Ergo.

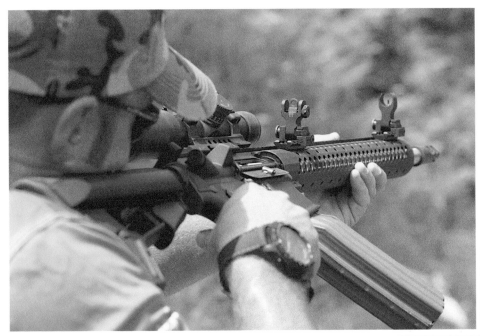

(left) Samson Manufacturing's Upgrade Kit features offset iron sights, along with the company's extremely popular Evolution rail system.

Samson Competition Rifle Upgrade Kit

At a retail price around $550, the Samson Manufacturing Rifle Upgrade Kit is touted to contain everything a shooter needs to get their rifle match ready. The kit contains a 15-inch Evolution Rail, Quick Flip Front and Rear Sights, Enhanced Low Profile Gas Block, Evolution QD sling point, and Samson Field Survivor tool.

(middle right) John Bagakis takes on long-range rifle targets from an awkward firing position during the 2010 3GN Championship.

(right) Don Bednorz transitions out of a prone rifle position during the 2010 3GN Championship.

SHOT

THE GUNS

Depending on the division in which one competes, there are several different shotgun platforms. In Open, for example, the box magazine-fed Saiga shotgun has become extremely popular, often heavily customized to achieve the desired results. Meanwhile, in Heavy Metal, where the pump-action is still king, Remington 870s, Mossberg 500s, old Winchester 1200s, and Benelli Novas all see good action. But the volume of shotgunning comes down in Tactical Optics, where the Benelli M2, FNH USA SLP, and Remingtons, both old 1100s and the new VersaMax, are all popular on the firing line.

"Remington and Benelli are top of the list," said Bruce Piatt. "FNs will be there soon, too, as will the Saiga box-fed shotguns.

"There are two main differences between Remingtons and Benellis," Piatt explained. "Remingtons are all steel, thus heavier, which can be good and bad. The extra weight sucks up recoil, but some say it makes it harder to handle or swing quickly. Benellis and FNs use alloy frames and are lighter, making them kick harder but swing faster. I guess it comes down to personal preference."

The shotgun game, for many beginning 3-gunners, is an eye-opening experience. Never before have most been subjected to loading a shotgun in this manner, under the stress of the clock. A first-time 3-gunner often

(right) A group of shooters pre-load their shotgun tubes prior to running a stage at the 2011 Texas Multi-Gun Championship.

looks as though they were leaving a trail of breadcrumbs to follow through the forest, littering the range bay with shotshells, as they amble through the course; then again, most first-timers are loading out of their trouser pockets or, at best, borrowed shell caddies, either way a nearly futile exercise without practice beforehand. But, that's okay, because I've heard some of the very best 3-gunners in the game relate similar stories about their first attempt at practical shotgunning (which means there's at least hope for the rest of us).

Shotgun use in 3-gun, and this varies depending on the venue, also includes several sub-games. It's not just load your shotgun and point it at every target you might face. Instead, there are subtleties that break down the shotgun game into distinct parts.

The most common component of shotgun courses is regular

(above) Brian Vaught runs an all-shotgun stage at the 2011 Kentucky State Multi-Gun Championships. Note the volume of shell caddies.

(left) Once the most popular shotgun in the sport, you still see a few Remington 1100s in the mix at matches.

old birdshot. The overwhelming majority of all targets faced will be engaged with standard No. 7½ shot, be it steel knock-over targets, steel poppers, Texas Stars, stationary clay targets, aerial clay birds, or clays affixed to moving target apparatus.

Distances vary, and so, too, will the chokes used to neutralize targets effectively. Improved Cylinder and Modified are very common, but others regularly use Light Modified and even Skeet. Their use varies from shooter to shooter, and it's a formula best arrived upon by the individual competitor's skill level and patterning the loads at distance.

Popular in both IPSC-style shotgun and 3-gun matches alike, buckshot, though not common, can be required. Slugs, on the other hand, have become a staple for many major 3-gun matches, with distances bordering on the ridiculous, out to 100 yards or more at some Outlaw matches. In any event, slug shots are very much a part of today's 3-gun game, and if you plan to shoot a major, and in some cases even a local club match, you had better know where your slug impacts out 75 yards or more to be competitive.

The biggest roadblock with the shotgun for new shooters is the act of loading. There are three common techniques employed today by top 3-gun shooters. They are the weak-hand reload, the strong-hand reload, and the two-by, or TWinS load.

Weak-Hand Reload

The weak-hand shotgun reload is, with few exceptions, the most dominant shotgun loading technique in the sport of 3-gun. While FN's Dave Neth is fast and furious, and AMU's Daniel Horner nearly unbeatable—both of whom load with the strong hand—weak-hand loading is still the winning technique most often used. Watch Taran Butler, Rob Romero, or Keith Garcia, and you'll see there is little doubt how devastatingly fast the weak-hand reload can be.

It all started with Kurt Miller, the "Father of the Weak-Hand Reload." Before he started dominating on the 3-gun fields—Miller is one of the most accomplished iron sight shooters in the sport—he served as a U.S. Marine, before taking a teaching position at Colonel Jeff Cooper's famed Gunsite Academy, in Arizona. It was there that the emerging practical shooter took a rigid defensive technique and refined it into what it is today.

"I didn't invent weak-hand loading," Miller explained. "It was a Gunsite technique, but they only loaded one shell at a time, stressing the need to keep the weapon on the shoulder. Eddie Rhodes was the first guy I ever saw who grabbed three shells at a time. From there, I practiced and got it to the level it is today."

As the sport evolved, so, too, did the importance of shotgun loading. Ultimately, shotgun round counts swelled in stage designs. While most top shooters often shot at similar speeds, the art of loading a shotgun within courses of fire began to separate the pack. When Miller began winning major 3-gun matches utilizing his 'new' loading technique, competitors took notice. Since then, Miller has taught nearly anyone who'll listen.

"I perfected it and designed the core of how to teach it, and then, of course, started winning with it," Miller said. "Being vocal about how good this system was got me to be the 'father' of the weak-hand load!"

When shooting a 3-gun match, you never know what match directors will throw at you. Shotgun targets can be pre-

sented in all manners, and there are always many ways in which to attack those stages. Nevertheless, when a match director wants to put you in an alterna-

(top) Ben Powell grabs shells while conducting a weak-hand reload.

(middle and bottom) Rob Romero conducts a weak-hand shotgun reload during the 2011 Rocky Mountain 3-Gun.

Kurt Miller, considered the father of the weak-hand reload, runs his Benelli during the 2010 Midwest 3-Gun Championship.

tive shooting or loading position, they usually have the means to do so. All this translates into the need to have many tools within one's shooting box. For shotgun loading, that means the ability to load from any position.

"Weak-hand loading is the most versatile and, in most cases, fastest method of loading the shotgun," Miller said. "It can be done with equal speed from any position, from prone, kneeling, sitting, standing, and on a dead run. It lets me see where I'm going and all the area around the gun instead of staring at an up-side down shotgun port."

The most impressive gain from using the weak-hand method is the ability to load while keeping the gun in the shoulder. I've seen shooters such as Miller, Jeff Cramblit, and Trapr Swonson actually continue to move with

the gun in the shoulder, while simultaneously breaking shots and pulling shells from the caddy. It's awesome to watch a top pro run a gun this way. More importantly, it shaves crucial seconds.

"For a 3-gunner, it's a very critical skill, in my opinion, to keep the gun at the shoulder during reload," Miller said. "It takes at least an extra 1½ to two seconds to drop the shotgun from the shoulder and, after loading, re-shoulder and re-index the target—wasted time! The other part is, as you load, you can re-engage a missed target without having to stop your loading process. Just point the shouldered shotgun at the target and shoot it with your strong hand only.

"I saved myself three to five seconds at the Texas State 3-Gun match with just this tactic," Miller continued. "I was just starting to step out of a port to load and run to the next position, when I noticed the steel plate I'd previously engaged was not impressed by my pattern on it,

so, as I grabbed the four shells to load to the next position, I merely aimed the gun at the target one-handed, pressed the trigger, and got the plate while continuing my loading."

The weak-hand reload begins with the grab. By using the wall of the shellcaddy as a guide, shooters can establish a reference point from which to build muscle memory, ensuring a clean, smooth grab every time.

"When you reach for the first shells, use your middle finger to reach down the side of the shell caddy closest to your weak side," Miller said. "Use it to start the grab by pushing it in between the amount of shells you are comfortable grabbing, which should be three to four. Next, your thumb drops around the top of the shell stack, you slide your middle finger right up along the side of the caddy and the shells stack into your hand."

According to Miller, many inexperienced shooters often make

(above) Kurt Miller, considered the father of the weak-hand reload, tops off his shotgun during a stage at the 2011 Rocky Mountain 3-Gun.

(left) Mark Hanish executes a weak-hand shotgun reload, the most popular style for shotgun loading in 3-gun.

In review, the weak-hand reload, as taught by Miller, has three main points.

"The three main points of weak-hand loading are to get a good consistent grab on the shells from the carrier, keep your loading thumb in contact with the shotgun lifter or loading port, and don't try to keep the shells flat to the gun!" Miller emphasized.

Practice, of course, is the key to building this skill set. However, Miller does not recommend spending hours on end of stuffing shells into your gun. Instead, 15 minutes of "good practice" will serve shooters better.

"Once you have the basic skills of weak-hand loading, dry practice with dummy rounds no more than 15 minutes at a time," Miller said. "This is the optimal time for letting your hand and brain learn the skill without overtaxing and fatigue. Anything more than this will actually hinder what you do. For most folks, a 15-minute session should be akin to loading around seven to 10 sets of eight shells—no more!

Strong-Hand Reloads

While Miller's weak-hand load is the most dominant method employed, it is by no means the only way to get the job done. For years, Bennie Cooley, a top 3-gun competitor, has utilized a strong-hand reload in competition. Dave Neth used a similar method for years, and his "tactical slide" method is one now copied by others in the sport.

Neth's technique calls for competitors to use the weak hand to position the shotgun butt on the shoulder with a clear view of the loading port. From there,

the mistake of attempting to hold all four rounds flat in their hand. This usually ends in shells bouncing on the ground, with rounds coming out of their owner's grip, through the 'back door,' if you will.

"Shell retention is the key here, and too many folks try to keep all the shells flat in their hand, kind of like laying all four shells on the table," Miller said. "This is where most folks run into trouble. For shell containment, let the lower two fingers naturally curl in below the rims of the shells you just grabbed, kind of like if you were trying to hold three golf balls without dropping them. Now the shells

won't fall out of your hand, and they are much easier to roll into the loading port."

Finally, maintaining contact with gun during the interim between loading shells is critical to building speed. Having to reestablish the index point robs competitors of the smoothness exhibited by top pros such as Miller.

"When you get to the load, remember to keep your loading thumb in contact with the lifter or loading port," Miller said. "This keeps you from loading a shell and then dropping your hand away and having to build the index all over again."

one simply uses the strong hand to grab shells, either off a side-saddle carrier, an arm sleeve, or a belt caddy and load the shell into the gun.

"When I'm ready to load the shotgun, from the shooting position I turn the gun sideways and slide it up my shoulder," Neth said. "That allows me to control the muzzle with (my weak hand), and it frees up my strong hand. From here, I'll simply grab my shells off the side saddle and load."

If loading from the side saddle or arm band, shells are grabbed and loaded one at a time into the gun. While not practical from a belt-worn shell caddy, the proximity of the shells riding either on the gun or in a sleeve on the weak arm, make this move quick and competitive.

One strong point of Miller's weak-hand method is that it gives competitors the ability to load while keeping the gun in the shoulder. I've seen Miller,

Jeff Cramblit, and others execute this move while traversing a stage, going to the caddy and loading without ever bringing the gun out of the shoulder—an impressive skill. This cannot be achieved doing Neth's slide method, yet he remains one of the fastest competitors with a shotgun in all of 3-gun. With the tactical slide, Neth needs only to push the gun back off the shoulder to have it quickly returned to action.

"By pushing my support hand back out and pointing at the target, it brings the gun right off my shoulder and back on target," Neth said.

A second method for conducting a strong-hand reload, one often employed by Neth and used exclusively by Daniel Horner, involves taking the weak hand, which is already on the fore-end, and using it to simply roll the shotgun inboard. The strong hand is then used to acquire shells from a belt caddy and load the shotgun in a manner similar to Miller's weak-hand method.

"The other method I like to use is a strong-hand reload from a shell caddy off my belt," Neth said. "This requires you to grab four shells at once and bring them up. The shotgun comes underneath your arm, and you simply load one round at a time while keeping the muzzle pointed downrange and towards the target."

The Load-Two

The weak- and strong-hand reloads, while distinct from each

While the weak-hand is the most used, many top competitors such as Bruce Piatt still use a strong-hand shotgun reload.

other, are variations on at least a similar theme. However, the "two-by" or "load-two" technique is something entirely new.

During the 2010 Pan American IPSC Shotgun Championship at the Rockcastle Shooting Center, in a Level IV match that drew an international field, a fresh shotgun loading technique landed on American shores via the European contingent. Not only was it something radical and new to many American shooters, it was fast, especially in the hands of the Italians, who were especially strong in the match.

"Two of the Italian shooters would hold up their gun's loading gate and draw two shells at a time between their index and middle fingers, dropping one on the loading gate and thumbing it and the second one into the magazine tube, one behind the other," said Patrick Kelley, whose U.S. Standard Manual team took first place.

While several European competitors used a belt system to space out the rounds in pairs, others used homemade chest rigs that carried the shells stacked vertically. For several of the American shooters, the unique shell caddy turned heads first, but the loading technique itself was what really caught their attention.

"I did not get to see the so-called 'suicide bomber' vests in action, but three of the Italian shooters were using a technique that I found very interesting, and they were certainly fast," said U.S. Standard Manual team member Joe Satterfield. "They would pull two shells off their belt strong hand and use the nose of one to push the other into the magazine. I have played with it some since I got

A new type of shotgun load landed on American shores via Italy during the 2010 Pan American Shotgun Championships.

home and definitely think there is some potential there."

Word of the technique and new gear spread like wildfire through the 3-gun community. Within months, a couple different products were on the market, and now the technique is starting to find some favor with 3-gun competitors.

"It's a great way for newer shooters to learn to load a shotgun and be as competitive as seasoned professionals that are doing the weak-hand or strong-hand reload," said Noveske's Jansen Jones.

While many new shooters struggle with learning to grab four shells at one time and manipulate them into the shotgun, Jones and other 3-gunners have seen the European technique as an easier method to learn quickly. The load-two technique simplifies the loading process down into three easy steps.

"There are, in my opinion, three keys," Jansen Jones said. "Make sure you have the buttstock on your shoulder, the loading port at an angle where you can see it, and then get a nice, smooth grab. Watch the shells go in—the key is to not take your eyes off the shells. The first shell drops on the lifter, the second shell pushes it in."

The Drill

In 3-gun competition, winning with a shotgun, on most stages, boils down to loading skills. The shooter who does it the smoothest and fastest oftentimes wins the stage. The heavier the stage's round count, the more critical solid shotgun loading skills become. Here's a drill the pros practice to get themselves ready for a match.

When using a shotgun with an eight-round magazine tube, start by loading two rounds in the gun, one of those in the chamber. At the start signal, engage one target, and then begin covering ground to the next target. While moving, load eight rounds into the gun.

For most competitors, this drill requires going to their belt caddy two times, grabbing four rounds at a time. If using the load-two or TWinS system, the competitor will be required to make four moves to the shell holder. Remember, this isn't a tactical drill, so you don't have to keep your eyes downrange.

Find the caddy on your belt, and watch those rounds as you feed them into the gun.

"You already know what your footing is going to be," said champion 3-gunner Bruce Piatt. "The details of the loading process are what make you fast. Pay attention to how you get the shells each time."

Once all eight rounds are loaded into the tube, engage your second target (note that, if using a standard timer, the time elapsed between the two shots will give you your loading time). Change up the drill by going left to right, then right to left, forward and even backward—every type of movement will be thrown into a 3-gun stage at one point or another.

During a match, when working out a stage plan, loading a shotgun goes hand-in-hand with the number of shots that have to be fired and how much real estate needs to be covered until the next shot. The best 3-gunners manage to hit their reloads in that amount of space and time.

"In competition, if your feet are moving, you should be loading," Piatt said. "Keep it in multiples of what you can grab and load."

When moving, always know where downrange is and never break the 180-degree line, which would flag other competitors behind you. Not only is that extremely unsafe, it's an immediate disqualification from the match. So in practice, be conscious of where you're moving and where the gun has to be pointed—all while concentrating on making smooth, fast loads.

Load all eight and break the shots in 10 seconds and you've achieved a good benchmark of time from which to begin. Do it as fast as Bruce Piatt and other top pros, and you're going to be down in the five-second range or below—and that's *smokin'* fast.

Regardless the shotgun drill or practice you employ, most top shooters teach to go slowly first, building the muscle memory of the perfect load, not a fast load. Once the fundamentals are established, speed can be built from there.

"One of the things that's really important in 3-gun shooting is to practice your shotgun loading," said Keith Garcia. "I'll start off with the gun shouldered in position, drop it down to where I reload from, acquire my shells and feed them in, keeping my hand position where I want it, then shoulder the gun, seeing what it looks and feels like to do it right. That way, when I speed it up, my body already knows what it's supposed to be doing, I'm just going to try and do it faster. My objective at the end of a short training session is to put myself on the spot. I'm thinking to myself, *You've got one load, Keith—this is the one you've got to make under pressure for the match and pull it off.* That kind of load will win you stages."

The Guns

Let's talk for a minute about the individual guns playing a major role in today's game of 3-gun.

FNH USA SLP Mark I

Over the last couple 3-gun seasons, no shotgun platform has likely enjoyed more explosive growth in use than the FNH SLP. The Mark I variant is the model of choice in 3-gun, com-

ing ready right out of the box for high-level 3-gun competition.

Although the line was originally developed for the tactical community, and since so many practical and tactical features overlap, the SLP needs no after-market accessories or modifications to compete with it. With a 3-inch chamber, the gas-operated semi-auto reliably functions on 2¾-inch shells. Two pistons come with the gun, one of which FN claims is optimized to run on lighter target loads.

The eight-plus-one tubular magazine capacity is standard fare for running in all but the Open division, and a low-profile, adjustable folding rear sight blade, matched with a fiber optic front, is suitable for both slugs and shot. Simply raise the folded rear when a stage has

For the last few seasons, no other shotgun has gained ground on Benelli in popularity more than the FNH USA SLP.

slugs incorporated, and you can leave it up without worry to engage any birdshot targets that may be mixed in.

Weighing in at 8.2 pounds, the FN sits in the middle of typical 3-gun shotguns—heavier than a Benelli, yet lighter than a Remington 1100. It wears a 22-inch barrel, crossbolt safety, steel sling swivels, and a matte black finish for a package that has become ubiquitous in the racks of major 3-gun matches across the country.

SLP Mark I Competition

While the SLP was gaining traction within the 3-gun community, FNH went a step further last year with the debut of the FN SLP Mark I Competition. The same shotgun used by Team FNH USA and featured in the 3-Gun Nation Shoot-Off, the Mark I Competition features a blue anodized receiver emblazoned with "TEAM FNH USA."

The FN SLP is arguably second only to Benelli in terms of popularity on the national 3-gun landscape.

Benelli M2/Salient Arms Modified

The Benelli M2 has long been a favored choice among 3-gunners. The recoil-operated guns are extremely light and lively, and they just seem to flat out run. The only problem with it is that Benelli has seldom offered one straight from the factory that didn't need some extra work to make it competition ready—mostly in the form of an extended magazine tube. Yet, this did little to deter competitors from snatching up Benellis and sending them off to gunsmiths.

In 2010, Salient Arms, a California custom shop, made a lot of noise, when it started selling highly modified Benelli M2 shotguns. In truth, it wasn't that all the modifications employed on the Salient version were new, as gunsmiths such as Benny Hill and others had been turning out tricked Benellis for some time. But the Salient package had an appeal that launched a major wave in 3-gun.

Part of it was that, unlike those from some gunsmiths, the Salient versions were finely finished and looked as good as they shot. Another factor was the involvement of Taran Butler, one of the top competitors in the sport.

"Salient Arms International is a division of Salient Security Services, which is a diversi- fied corporation that has been providing executive and personal protection services to VIPs and celebrities all over the U.S. and abroad," said Tony Pignato of Velocity Shooter, one of Salient's early dealers. "Rob Melhorn and Fred Lindley are the key members of the Salient Arms International firearms production division and have more than 30 years of combined experience in custom and competition firearms. Both Rob and Fred have been Taran Butler's gunsmiths since the beginning of his professional shooting career. Taran is also a professional consultant to Salient Arms, specifically for the competition firearms production. With his numerous years of experience and product knowledge, he was a perfect choice for USPSA/

Tricked out Benelli M2s are a favorite among many 3-gun competitors.

IPSC and multi-gun product development.

"My company, Velocity Shooter, was brought in to provide a link from the manufacture to direct customer sales. As Salient Arms International's primary source for product purchase, I also provide guidance on marketing and retail relations, based on my experiences with the competition and firearms industry," Pignato stated.

Within a matter of what seemed like months, top competitors such as Kurt Miller and Rob Romero joined Butler in running a Salient Arms Benelli. And why not? It had a collection of accessories and modifications that had become standard in 3-gun competition.

Salient upgraded the safety button, magazine tube and nut, and added an Arredondo oversized carrier release bar. Internally, the bolt carrier, extractor, trigger, and chamber were all enhanced or modified.

"We use a DMW (Dave Metal Works) magazine tube and magazine nut built to our specifications, because of the proven product performance and quality craftsmanship; the Benelli magazine extension clamp, because it provides quality, ease of removal, and integration into our performance platform; and Wolff magazine springs, because of their high quality and durability," said Pignato.

"The Salient Benelli M2 has a much better trigger pull, a match trigger," Butler said. "It's a faster loading gun—it's like glass, and your thumb doesn't get caught on that half-moon cutout the factory lift gate has. When the bolt recovers, because it's lighter, it doesn't dip

Ben Fortin runs his Benelli during a stage at the 2011 Midwest 3-Gun Championship.

the front sight at all. And, if the bolt is partly out of battery, you can still put a round in the tube without it getting seized up in the gun and causing a catastrophic jam."

Benelli Performance Shop M2 3-Gun

The effect of the Salient M2 must not have been lost on Benelli, which, by 2011, had finally jumped into the sport by sponsoring its first 3-gun team, with Taran Butler chief among it. In 2012, Benelli followed that up with the introduction of the Performance Shop M2 3-Gun.

Benelli's Performance Shop M2 utilizes a Nordic Components Speed Button bolt release and an oversized tactical bolt handle. An eight-shot magazine extension increases capacity to division standards, while a Teflon-coated magazine follower minimizes internal hanging or over-compression of the magazine spring. Additionally, the loading port is widened, with all sharp edges beveled; combined with the modified carrier, greatly enhances the ease of

loading. Weighing 7.2 pounds, the Performance Shop M2 is light and nimble, with a 21-inch barrel that utilizes a fiber optic sight suitable for slug use.

Now, hold your breath—the Performance Shop M2 3-Gun carries a suggested retail of nearly $2,700. But, considering the cost of a new M2, combined with the custom features included in this package, that price isn't nearly as obscene as it might look at first glance.

Remington VersaMax Tactical

The new Remington VersaMax Tactical, though marketed toward law enforcement and home-defense, is nevertheless out-of-the-box-ready for 3-gun competition. Utilizing Remington's new "Versa Port" gas system, the VersaMax is billed as being able to handle any type of shotshell on the market.

"The heart of the VersaMax is the Versa Port gas system,"

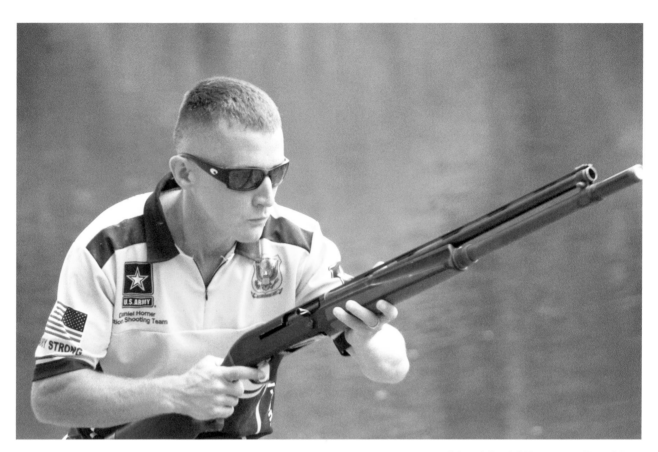

said Brian Lasley, Shotgun Product Manager at Remington. "This unique gas system auto-regulates the gas pressure, based on the length of the shell being used, for flawless cycling of all 12-gauge loads."

An eight-plus-one magazine makes the VersaMax suitable for division requirements, while an oversized bolt release and button are also well suited for competition. However, it's the internal design that has received the lion's share of attention since the shotgun's release, as Remington claims the system requires little cleaning to maintain reliability.

"With its self-cleaning design, the Versa Port gas system stands ready to cycle hundreds of rounds with minimal cleaning, an amazing testament to its reliability," Lasley said.

Bruce Piatt, Robby Johnson, and Daniel Horner are among a select group of 3-gun pros already running the VeraMax in competition. By all accounts, each of them plan on running one for some time to come.

(above) Daniel Horner readies with his Remington VersaMax, which made serious waves in the 3-gun world in 2011.

(below) The pump-action shotgun, this one a Mossberg 590, still has a home in 3-gun in the Heavy Metal division.

Mossberg JM Pro Series 930 Tactical Class

With Mossberg's release of the JM Pro Series shotguns, the company is attempting to leverage the winning name of top 3-gun pro Jerry Miculek alongside the solid design of the Mossberg 930 line of semi-automatics. By all accounts, that should be a formula for success.

The heart of the 930 platform is its dual-vent operating system that helps mitigate the forces of recoil in this gas-operated design. The anodized receiver incorporates a chamfered loading port, which should aid in loading.

The only major manufacturer to offer a 10-shot variant straight from the factory (along with a nine-shot version), Mossberg is clearly listening to Miculek as to what can help stand it apart from what is quickly becoming a crowded field of shotguns marketed for 3-gun competition. The 10-shot Tactical Class (nine-plus-one capacity) features a 24-inch vent rib barrel, while the nine-shot version (eight-plus-one capacity) wears a 22-inch vent rib barrel.

Benelli Nova

Likely the most common choice among top pump-action shotgun users in 3-gun, many shooters got a real treat watching the Italian team running these guns during the 2010 Pan American Shotgun Championship at the Rockcastle Shooting Center. Their Standard Manual team was extremely impressive with the Nova.

In America, Patrick Kelley has been thought of as this country's best pump-action shotgunner for several years. Kelley, who spent much of his shooting career running an out-of-production Win-

A competitor engages targets with a pump-action shotgun during the 2011 FNH USA 3-Gun Championship.

chester 1300 Camp Defender in Heavy Metal matches, switched to the Benelli Nova last season as part of his new sponsorship from Benelli USA.

Though Benelli markets a Tactical model, in truth, most Heavy Metal shooters pick up a used field model and then customize it to suit their need, most notably with a magazine extension tube from Nordic Components and other accessory makers.

Remington 870 and Mossberg 500

While more veteran shooters may use the Nova, sheer volume still belongs to the Remington 870. That, as much as anything, is simply a reflection of the market itself. Also in the mix is the Mossberg 500. Each of these shotguns has been produced in countless variations over the years, and there is a wide mix of customized former field models and factory-fresh tactical variants from both brands currently enjoying good use in 3-gun.

Box Magazine-Fed Shotguns

The holy grail of shotgunning is the absolutely reliable, yet affordable box magazine-fed shotgun design. In the imported Saiga 12 shotguns, there is certainly affordability, with guns retailing from Russian American Armory for around the price of a new polymer-framed pistol and even some pump-action shotguns. However, to make one run reliably enough for competition, the Saiga's price balloons into one more closely represented by an Open-style 2011 pistol.

Nevertheless, customized Saiga shotguns from R&R and Firebird Precision, among a select few others, have grown steadily in use among Open shooters. Firebird also unveiled a new twist on the box magazine-fed shotgun at the 2012 SHOT Show, when it introduced its highly tuned version of the Akdal MKA 1919, a Turkish import manufactured by Akdal Arms. Externally, the Firebird's improved 1919 is all AR-15, in terms of button and controls, which will sit well with most 3-gunners. Internally, the 1919 more closely resembles a Remington 1100, which has been successful in 3-gun since the days of SOF. Amazingly, the Firebird 1919 retails for $1,800—if this guns runs anywhere close to as reliably as a tuned Saiga, and for a fraction of the cost, the balance of power in Open shotguns could be at the beginning of a major shift.

(right) The MKA 1919, after being worked over by Firebird Precision, could seriously challenge the Saiga in the Open division.

(below) Kay Miculek, competing in the Open division, runs a Saiga shotgun during a match.

(opposite) Heavily customized Saiga shotguns, from makers such as R&R, are very popular in the Open division.

THE TOLS

For many of the sport's very best competitors, action pistol shooting is where they cut their teeth. Though that trend seems to be shifting a bit, with more shooters coming straight into 3-gun than ever before, pistol shooters still make up the majority of the talent. One reason for that is access. More local clubs, for a much greater time period, have run pistol matches on a consistent basis. They're easier to staff, easier to set up and take down, and even for the competitors themselves, a weekend pistol match is more affordable and convenient.

"I think the sheer fact that someone has excelled at USPSA pistol shooting shows that they are well grounded in the basic fundamentals of shooting," said champion 3-gun and pistol competitor Bruce Piatt. "Combining shooting, reloading, moving, and negotiating obstacles or complex courses of fire, all while balancing accuracy and time on the clock, is the foundation to a great shooter—no matter what the sport. If you had the drive and ability to learn to do all those things in a course of fire, then you have the ability to adjust to any shooting situation."

Pistol shooting remains the hardest skill sets to master within 3-gun. Sure, shotgun loading is a difficult and foreign task for nearly every new 3-gun shooter, and long-range rifle has a science to it that can only be understood with time on the range. Yet, pistol shooting maintains the highest degree of difficulty, simply because it's the least forgiving tool of the trade. It's often said matches are won with rifle shooting or shotgun loading—and they can only be lost with a pistol.

At matches such as Superstition Mountain Mystery 3-Gun, the pistol game is a wide open, blazing-fast affair.

"The way most matches are presented now, you can't win a match as a result of pistol," Piatt said. "If the match staff presents a lot of small distant targets with a lot more no-shoot penalty opportunities, then a match could be *swayed* by the best pistol shooter. I doubt it will ever come to that point, though, because if it was that difficult for the top guys, imagine how the middle of the pack is going to feel driving home after such a match!"

Obviously smaller and lighter by comparison to rifles and shotguns, and with a drastically decreased sighting radius, a competitor is forced to be more solid in the fundamentals to run a pistol well. Long-range rifle, in terms of 3-gun shooting, certainly requires discipline in breathing, position, and trigger control, but shooters seem to be able to apply that skill set more quickly with a rifle. Jerk the

trigger on a pistol at close-range paper, on the other hand, and an "A" hit turns into a "C." And a bad trigger pull on even close-range steel? That's likely to be a miss altogether.

"Having the ability to consistently hit your target, no matter what the conditions, is what will make someone a successful 3-gun pistol shooter," Piatt said. "Now, if you can do it with speed, then you'll be a *great* 3-gun pistol shooter.

"Get to the range and experiment. Don't be afraid to change something every time you practice. Doing the same things over and over without experimentation will usually get you to a plateau. Change your grip pressure or trigger finger placement, anything. You might go right back to what you're doing now, but you would have learned what works and doesn't work for you."

At the highest level of competition, there is often very little that separates the winner from the rest of the pack. To that end, each match must be approached differently, depending on the challenge presented by the match director.

"Depending on the match, with smaller targets at distance, the most *accurate* shooter with the least misses is usually going to gain some ground," Piatt said. "When there are big, close targets with movement, then the *faster* shooter is going to take the lead. I just go out there and do my best, no matter what the challenge."

The latest trend challenging competitors is the use of small, reactive steel targets, often placed at extremely long-range pistol distances. While this type of stage design serves several purposes, it has one monumental effect—it forces competitors, sometimes right in

the middle of an all-out run-and-gun stage, to slow down and get a good trigger press for accuracy.

Piatt agrees. "Yes, that has been the trend lately," he said. "I think the match directors were initially trying to minimize the logistics of buying targets and the labor of scoring paper. You have to remember that, especially if it's a rainy day, using bags over paper targets and keeping the hole pasters on the targets can add hours to a match. Rain, snow, or wind don't have too much effect on a piece of steel. Cost-wise, compared to buying targets, tape, and sticks for every match, the initial larger cost of the steel will pay for itself over the years. But whether or not it's about cost, this type of target presentation lends itself well to a shooter with more of an accuracy based foundation."

Like most 3-gun competitors,

Piatt, a New Jersey law enforcement officer and family man, has the same time constraints that limit most folks' time on the range. Because of that, his pistol training is focused, deliberate, and efficient.

"First of all, considering my work and family schedule, my practice sessions are few and far between," Piatt said. "I'll always start off with a zero check, then move right into some distance shooting. I'll shoot out to 50 yards, focusing on groups or hitting an eight-inch plate. Then I'll do some speed shooting on bigger targets, working on split times and target transitions at 10 and 15 yards. Then I'll continue the same drills, but do them on the move."

"I'll shoot a couple mags one-handed and weak-handed," Piatt continued. "No matter what I do, I'll always finish up my practice session back where I began—shooting some accuracy groups from distance, so that I leave the range with trigger control fresh on my mind."

Few are more qualified to speak on the intricacies of pistol shooting than Piatt. He's a five-time NRA Bianchi Cup Champion, the 2006 World NRA Action Pistol Champion, and a 17-time USPSA National Law Enforcement Division Champion, not to mention numerous championships in 3-gun and other disciplines. So I asked him, out of all the aspects of pistol shooting—stance, grip, trigger press, sights, splits, transitions, and on and on—what was the most important item one should focus on to make improvement for 3-gun? For Bruce, it all comes down to one thing—get the hits.

"As you mention, getting really good at split times and target transitions will shave tenths of seconds from your time," Piatt said. "Being accurate and missing less is going to shave *full* seconds off your time!"

"A lesson I learned many years ago came from a discussion I was part of with a group of well-known shooters, including the then-current winner of the Steel Challenge, Angelo Spagnoli," Piatt continued. "We were quizzing each other on how he pulled off the win, and he claimed, and I will quote it as best I can remember, 'I didn't shoot faster than anyone out there, I just missed less.' That statement stuck with me, and I still follow that rationale to this day.

"Case in point was the 2010 3-Gun Nation Final Shoot-Off. I had to shoot against the likes of Jerry Miculek, Taran Butler,

While the Weaver stance and grip were the founding principals of action shooting, today's top competitors utilize more of a thumbs-forward grip and a forward-facing isosceles-type stance.

and Daniel Horner, knowing all the while that every one of them is faster than me 90 percent of the time. Following this 'miss less' mind-set allowed me to remain calm and just stick to what I know I can do, and that is be accurate. It worked for me. I finished second behind Horner and took home $10,000 to prove it."

Practical Pistols

With the surge in all things black gun and concealed carry, the pistol market, much like those for AR-15s and tactical-style shotguns, has never been stronger. But, for one interested in getting into 3-gun, walking into a gun shop with a wad of cash in the pocket can be intimidating.

"My advice for new 3-gun shooters trying to choose a pistol is not to rush it," Piatt said. "Come shoot with whatever gun you already have and are comfortable shooting, be it an out-of-the-box 1911 or one of the myriad plastic frame, striker-fired defensive guns. Just get out to the range and shoot some 3-gun. Pay attention to what others are shooting, and don't

be afraid to ask if you can try somebody's gun. That way you will invest your money wisely or find out what you already have will do just fine."

The 2011

For the guys and gals who play this game well, a majority have invested heavily in their pistol. Highly customized 2011 pistols most often fill the hands of match winners. You by no means have to run a 2011 to be competitive in 3-gun, but it's futile to argue that most top shooters use something else.

STI is likely the leader in this category, with varying levels of double-stacked 9mm or .38 Super models, and even guns in .40 S&W seeing use in competition. Caspian Arms, with its signature cast frames, are a favorite among some custom pistolsmiths, and companies such as Infinity, Bedell, Freedom Gunworks, and Accurate Iron are just but a sample of the many custom shops currently turning out quality 2011s suitable for 3-gun competition.

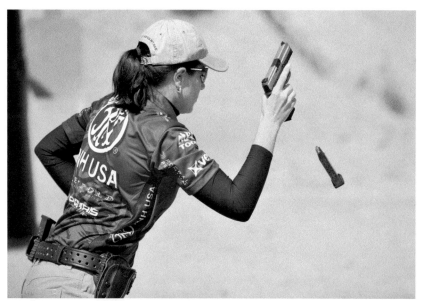

For those not ready to make the investment—some builds are in the $4,000 range—a quality polymer-framed pistol can still be had new for $500 to $600. Used models, of course, go for even less. And just as it is with 2011s, there is no shortage of smiths available to tune up these duty-style pistols to anyone's competition standards.

(top left) Junior shooter Katie Harris runs her 2011 pistol during the 2011 Rocky Mountain 3-Gun.

(top right) Tasha Hanish executes a pistol magazine reload during the 2011 Superstition Mountain Mystery 3-Gun.

(middle) Bruce Piatt runs a Caspian pistol at the Blue Ridge Mountain 3-Gun. Caspian's cast receivers are a popular choice for many custom pistolsmiths.

(bottom) Custom 2011-style semi-automatic pistols from makers such as STI, Infinity, and others are extremely popular in all but the most limited divisions of 3-gun.

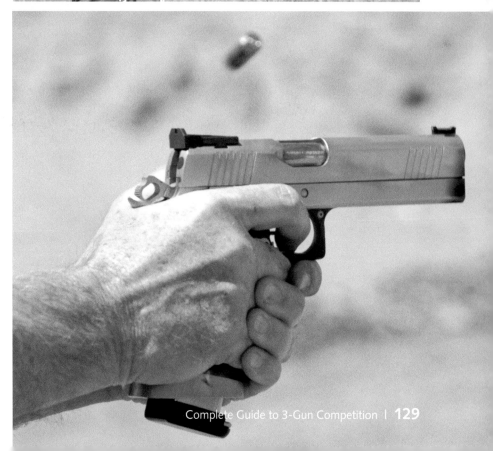

Glock 17/34

As it is in law enforcement and civilian sales, chances are the Glock is also the most-used handgun in 3-gun. Okay, maybe not necessarily among elite shooters, as most top 3-gunners use a 2011 or are tied to a particular sponsor, but definitely for the majority of other competitors. The Glock is a very popular choice.

Most Glocks you see on 3-gun firing lines are model G17s or G34s, both chambered in 9mm, the most common pistol chambering at Outlaw matches. At USPSA Multi-Gun Nationals and pistol competitions, where the power factor comes into play, the .40 S&W certainly cuts into 9mm use, making the G35 a popular choice for competitors who play in both arenas.

What can you say about a Glock at this point that hasn't already been said? Known for incredible reliability, Glocks are generally accurate enough to be competitive, yet affordable enough to be accessible to most shooters. If I were buying one today for Outlaw 3-gun competition, my choice would be the G34. The 5.31-inch barrel is superior to that of the G17, and the standard magazine capacity is an ample 17 rounds, while 19- and even 33-round magazines are available. Moreover, there is no shortage of aftermarket parts, holsters, and custom gunsmiths ready to work on the Glock.

FNH USA FNS

FNH USA launched a new striker-fired pistol during SHOT Show 2012, highlighted by the finalists using it in the 3-Gun Nation Championship Finale on January 18 (the same

time as the SHOT show). During that week, the FNS made quite an impression on the SHOT show floor, in the competition, and during a Smoke 'N' Hope stage set up for media and industry professionals prior to the Championship.

"The new FNS series was designed to be the most operator-friendly semi-auto pistols available, and intended to give America's law enforcement officers a decisive edge," said Ken Pfau, Senior Vice President of Law Enforcement and Commercial Sales for FNH USA. "After five years of design development and nearly a half-million rounds of testing, the

FNS stands ready for duty with any agency, large or small."

Rumored to be working on a five-inch competition model, as well, the early FNS has proven to be well suited to the 3-gun game, as demonstrated by members of Team FNH USA in competition. As such, a low bore axis makes the pistol easy to control, while interchangeable backstraps enable a semi-custom fit for each user.

The FNS features fully ambidextrous controls, while low-profile three-dot night sights are standard. In 9mm, the magazine capacity is 17 rounds, while the FNS-40 holds 14 rounds. A polymer frame and stainless steel barrel and slide round out the package.

Springfield XD(M) 5.25 Competition Series

Like Glocks, Springfield XD pistols have enjoyed a good amount of popularity in action shooting, including 3-gun. They are affordable, they shoot well, and they're consistently reliable, even under hard use.

The 5.25 brings some custom house-type touches to a factory offering. Lightning cuts in the slide reduce slide mass for faster cycling, while fully adjustable sights and fiber optic front enable shooters a better system with which to zero loads, as compared to the standard model XD.

(left) FNH USA FNX-9 semi-automatic pistols staged prior to a 3-Gun Nation Shoot-Off in 2010.

(below) Polymer-framed, duty-style semi-automatic pistols in 9 mm are very popular choices in 3-gun competition.

Internally, a match-grade steel barrel with a Melonite finish employs a fully supported ramp. In 9mm, the 5.25 delivers a 19-plus-one capacity.

Smith & Wesson M&P Pro

At a suggested retail of $670, the M&P Pro line, like the Springfield XD(M) 5.25, is billed as an enhanced model of the company's already successful duty-style line of polymer-framed pistols, in this case the M&P. As such, the M&P Pro is built to deliver many custom shop-type enhancements, yet maintain "stock" definitions for practical pistol shooting.

While those requirements are non-existent in 3-gun, the M&P Pro is nevertheless becoming a popular choice, simply because the pistol delivers a number of solid upgrades for a good price.

Upgraded fiber optic Novak sights, a five-inch barrel, and an improved trigger make the striker-fired Pro series competitive. The M&P Pro 9 has a magazine capacity of 17-plus-one, keeping it in line with other comparable pistols in this category.

(top) Running and gunning the pistol portion of 3-gun requires reloads on the move.

(right) Taran Butler, one of the top pistol shooters in 3-gun, rips though a stage at the 2011 ARFCOM-Rockcastle Pro Am.

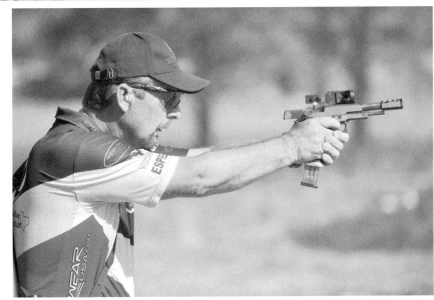

(top) Jeff Cramblit takes on pistol targets during the 2010 3GN Championship in Las Vegas.

(middle) Barry Dueck runs his pistol while competing in the Heavy Metal Optics division at the 2011 Rocky Mountain 3-Gun at the NRA Whittington Center in Raton, NM.

(left) Mike Voigt runs his Open pistol in competition.

Yamil R. Sued photo

THE OPTICS

Over the last few years, no area of 3-gun equipment has enjoyed as much technical advancement as has rifle scopes. With greater ranges of magnifications now available on scopes that deliver true one-power (1X) magnification at the lower end of the variable spectrum, rifle scopes have never been more well suited for 3-gun use.

The Weaver 1-5X delivers 1X at the low power end yet still magnifies out to 5X for long-range shooting.

Models with increased zoom range from Leupold, Swarovski, Bushnell, and others deliver top-end magnifications beyond the previous threshold of 4X on scopes that featured 1X at the bottom end. While monster top-end magnifications have been available for many years, it's the 1X that's the important part of the equation, as the sport of 3-gun demands the ability to shoot extremely close-range paper targets with a rifle.

Indeed, range bays themselves can be limited, making close-range targets a necessity, simply in order to get a sufficient amount of rifle shooting in. Moreover, fast-action close-range rifle, or "hosing," as it's referred to, is actually very much a part of the game. Trust me, there a few things more fun than getting on the trigger of a SCAR or AR-15 as fast as you possibly can, while running past a bank of paper targets 10 feet away.

Where scopes once maxed out at 4X, now 5X, 6X, and even 8X models are available, and they still include true 1X viewing. These bigger scopes are a boon in competitor's hands for long-range rifle shooting—a bigger boon for optics companies wanting to sell to tactical and practical shooters alike, as this is the hot trend in tactical-style optics.

The One-Powers (1X)

In 2010, new rules took over the Limited divisions of Outlaw 3-gun, with once-prohibited 1X optics suddenly approved for Tactical Iron and Heavy Metal in an effort to boost otherwise shrinking equipment classes. It worked, especially in Tactical Iron, at least in part because it immediately provided a new way to play the game. But, the development also benefited from the fact that there have never been more quality one-power optics.

Today's field of optics suitable for either secondary use on an Open gun or primary use in Limited divisions is dominated by reflex sights, including red dots, open-style reflex sights, and holographic sights. More recently, the conventional tube sight has been redesigned in the form of the Leupold Prismatic. Knowing the strengths of each, when combined with the primary duty of the shotgun, they can help shooters get the most out of sights that are diminutive in size but deliver big performance.

For nearly 10 years, the firearms industry watched as reflex sights turned from a curious anomaly to a staple of our soldiers' gear, with several makes and models used to good effect in Iraq and Afghanistan. Open competitor Mike Voigt is often credited for being one of the first, if not *the* first, to use a secondary sight on an optic in the sport of 3-gun—prior to similar use by the U.S. military.

Matt Burkett's Offset Sight Mount is suitable for mounting secondary optics on an Open rifle.

Aimpoint's Comp M4 has served with distinction with the military and has been used in 3-gun for years. A couple years ago, that technology was miniaturized into the revolutionary Micro series. A 1X red dot with unlimited eye relief, the Micro features a 4 MOA reticle and runs seemingly forever (five years continuous use at position No. 8, according to Aimpoint) on one three-volt lithium battery. Constructed of extruded aluminum and garbed in anodized black, the Micro is rugged.

The Micro weighs a scant three ounces and measures only 1.4 inches high, which keeps it (left) The new Burris FastFire III is one of several reflex-style sights common in the Open division.

(below l. to r.) Leupold DeltaPoint, EOTech, Leupold Prismatic, and Aimpoint Micro H1—Examples of 1X optics used in 3-gun.

(bottom) Reflex-style sights such as the Aimpoint Micro H1 are commonly used as secondary rifle optics and as primary shotgun and pistol sighting systems in the Open division.

low to the receiver and out of the way. It also comes set-up to mount directly to a Picatinny rail (common on most tactical shotguns), or easily added as an aftermarket accessory.

For a fraction of the price, Bushnell markets the TRS 1X25mm. I was pleasantly surprised, when I ran this optic atop a Ruger 10-22, shooting multiple steel targets at a Bushnell writer's conference. The TRS features a 3 MOA dot, multi-coated optics and an amber, high-contrast lens coating.

While the Micro and TRS are diminutive optics, the open-style reflex sights made famous by Docter are even smaller. In 3-gun, they dominate the field for secondary optics in Open division, with models by JP Enterprises, Trijicon, and Burris all popular. One of the newest entries into this field is Leupold's DeltaPoint, which has received excellent reviews from shooters in competition.

The DeltaPoint features a wider design compared to the lens housing common in most of its contemporaries. Leupold claims

Variable power scopes with a low power setting of 1X, such as the Burris 1-6X XTR, are popular in 3-gun.

this delivers up to 56-percent more usable field of view. Motion-activated, the DeltaPoint also continuously samples light conditions and uses that information to optimize reticle intensity. The DeltaPoint employs adjustment numbering to 120 MOA. The unit rides in a magnesium housing and is shockproof and waterproof. Weighing a mere 0.6 ounces and measuring 1.6 inches long, you'll never even know the DeltaPoint is there—that is, un-

til you see the red dot on target.

One of the hottest 1X optics recently introduced has been the Leupold Prismatic. I used the Prismatic often on M4 carbines as student in tactical training courses. The Prismatic is lightning fast for acquiring close-range targets, and top pros such as Kelly Neal and James Casanova have proven how accurate they can be at long range.

With the Prismatic, there is

The Leupold DeltaPoint is a great choice as a primary sighting system for any pistol or shotgun, or as a secondary rifle optic in the Open division.

(above) James Casanova hammers close-range rifle targets running a Leupold Prismatic in the Tactical Iron division.

much to make it stand apart from other reflex sights. First, it features the thickest main tube Leupold has ever built. The Prismatic also accepts a removable illumination module that delivers a red reticle with eight brightness settings, and an etched glass reticle lies within the 1X14mm scope, as well. When the illuminator is running, it superimposes over the existing etched glass, so, if a battery dies or the illuminator breaks under duress, there is always the etched reticle there. A competitor running a Prismatic is never out of the game.

The Leupold Prismatic delivers 1X capabilities in a tube design.

Amazingly, the EOTech holographic system has been around since 1996, with the first military/law enforcement model HWS produced in 2001. The EOTech works by projecting a holographic image back to the shooter. This system enables the unit to function even if the actual display window is broken. The technology of holography delivers all information required to reconstruct the image to every part of that window. As long as any part of it remains intact, unobstructed by mud, etc., then that reticle is visible and usable.

EOTech produces several variants today, both for tactical and sporting markets. Compared to the Micro or the DeltaPoint, EOTechs are much larger and heavier. Still, the system is lightning fast, the unit runs on simple AA batteries, and my unit is as close to indestructible as anything I've ever ran.

These are but a sample of the myriad options available today.

Whether for 3-gun competition, duty, or home-defense, the use of 1X optics on long guns is a growing trend. Bolt one on your shotgun or rifle, urn some ammo, and you'll know why.

Swarovski Z6i 1-6x24 BRT

No rifles cope made a bigger impact upon 3-gun than did the Swarovski Z6i, in 2011—it simply took the sport by storm. At the end of 2010, as these scopes were beginning to trickle out, they were extremely hard to find. Yet, I will never forget walking to a rack of rifles at Superstition, in 2011, where an entire squad had just placed their rifles in the rack. Out of 10 rifles staged there, eight of them wore the brand new Z6i—and there wasn't one sponsored shooter in the squad—amazing!

(right) One of the most popular scopes in 3-gun in 2011 was the Swarovski Z6i.

The Swarovski Z6i features a BRT reticle with multiple aimpoints past the initial zero.

The Z6i is attractive, in my opinion, and I shoot one for two major reasons besides its good looks, those being the reticle and the field of view. With the power knob wrenched down to 1X, the field of view, listed at 127 feet, is incredible. Where the competition is looking for individual targets, you are looking for entire arrays with the Z6i. The second really attractive feature is the BRT reticle, a combination of mil dots and vertical bullet drop compensation lines that offer an easy, basic formula for taking on targets out to extended ranges and which delivers five hold points beyond zero.

The BRT illuminated reticle features an illuminated dot, with both day and night settings. Also, Swarovski's website features an online ballistic calculator pre-programmed for standard .223 16-inch or 20-inch barrels and numerous factory loads, although you can put in handloads, as well. The calculator can also compute a competitor's drops from roughly 100 to 600 yards, with a typical load.

Leupold's new 1-6X should become a popular scope among 3-gunners in the near future.

Leupold Mark 6 1-6X20mm

Leupold's new Mark 6 1-6X20mm M6C1 debuted at SHOT 2012 to much fanfare, and with good reason. It delivers a lot of features sought by 3-gunners, but at a fraction of the price of much of the competition.

With its 6X zoom range, the Mark 6 delivers plenty of top-end magnification for most long-range targets. A wide field of view promotes fast target acquisition, especially at 1X. Available reticles include the CMR-762 and CMR-W 5.56, giving all optics divisions in 3-gun, including Heavy Metal Optics, a solid option.

"Whether you're on the battlefield or in a 3-gun competition, our new Mark 6 1-6X20mm rifle scope packs all the optical performance and versatility you need in an extremely compact, efficient package," said Kevin Trepa, Vice President, Tactical Division for Leupold & Stevens, Inc.

Weaver Tactical SPR 30mm Mount

The Weaver Tactical SPR (Special Purpose Rifle) 30mm Optics Mount places optics at an optimal height on AR-15-style rifles and is designed to fit the 30mm scope tubes prevalent in 3-gun competition. Constructed of 6061 T6 aluminum and hard-coat anodized, at $100 the SPR represents a significant value in this product category.

MGM Switchview

If 1X is the gas pedal stomped to the floor, and 6X is slowing down for accuracy, then the

MGM Switchview is the gear shifter to your rifle shooting. The MGM Switchview is a lever that enables you to quickly change the magnification of your scope. These are great for 3-gun rifles and long-range rifles alike. Being able to look for a target and then zoom in on it, in less than three seconds and without taking your head off the gun, is a huge advantage.

The MGM Switchview has an MSRP of $59.95 and is available to fit models from Leupold, Vortex, Burris, Millet, NightForce, Schmidt-Bender, Trijicon, and IOR Valdada.

Warne RAMP

Popular with Open and Limited division shooters alike, the Warne RAMP, for Rapid Acquisition Multi-Sight Platform, is a cantilever-style mounting solution designed to deliver proper scope height on AR-15-style rifles. The RAMP also features 45-degree offset rails, one on each side, for mounting secondary optics—perfect for Open shooters. For other divisions, these rails can be removed.

Warne RAMP mounts are constructed of 6000 series aluminum and feature No. 8 Torx fasteners. The RAMP is available for one-inch or 30mm scope tubes.

The RAMP Mount from Warne Scope Mounts features Picatinny rails at a 45-degree angle from the main optic—perfect for mounting a secondary optic.

The Weaver SPR Mount is a solid mounting system that is suitable for 3-gun use.

AMMU

THE AMMUNITION

The bane of every 3-gunner's existence is ammunition. For the most part, anyone who gets into 3-gun is a serious trigger-puller anyway. But, 3-gun is a new kind of "illness" that can only be treated again and again with ammo. As such, most veteran shooters handload their own rifle and pistol ammunition, in an effort to keep down costs. Say what you want about tuning loads to match the gun and all that. Not in this sport. For most 3-gunners, handloading is only about saving money.

Shotshells, on the other hand, are generally purchased in the form of factory ammunition. For the most part, whatever bulk pack of No. 7½ birdshot you can find on sale at Wal-Mart is plenty sufficient to shoot even a major Outlaw match. Some matches will call for buckshot from time to time, which does increase expense, but buckshot round counts for match play are almost universally kept on the low end. And, while there are maybe three guys in the sport, somewhere, who load their slugs (I haven't met them yet), with the cost of slugs added to some major matches, where trends are toward increased slug use and ridiculously long shots with them, handloading slugs may be brilliant after all! But, until then, loads such as Remington Managed Recoil will likely remain popular.

For those who don't like to handload (and there are a surprisingly significant number of 3-gunners who do not), factory ammunition for pistol and rifle use is most often ordered in bulk instead of purchased from the local gun shop or box store. Especially for competitors running duty-style pistols, plenty of Winchester white box, Remington UMC, Blazer, and other discounted brands are readily available and very much present on the firing line. Most Glocks, M&Ps, XDs and the like are pretty reliable with a wide range of pistol ammunition, unlike the tighter-fitting

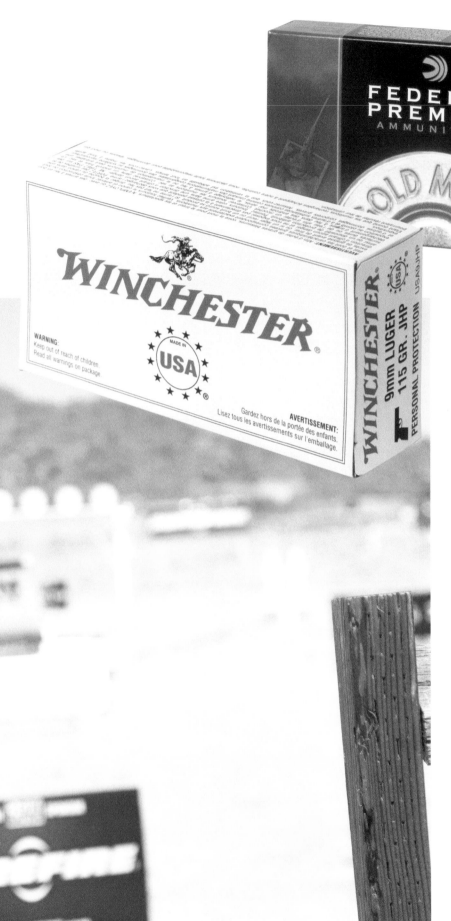

(above) While many shooters reload for practice, others still buy quality rifle ammunition such as Federal Gold Medal Match for game day.

(left) Value-priced ammunition is available from most major ammunition manufacturers, such as this 9mm load commonly referred to as "Winchester White Box."

(opposite) Federal Shotgun ammunition staged prior to a 3-Gun Nation Shoot-Off.

custom 2011s, which generally require better ammo for reliable operation.

Most competitors spend the majority of their ammunition allowance on quality rifle ammo. Even if they load or shoot lower-grade rounds for practice, many still purchase factory match-grade rifle ammunition for game day. These shooters continuously scour Brownells, Cheaper Than Dirt!, and elsewhere, looking for bulk deals or sales on their favorite loads. Following are a few affordable versions commonly seen in 3-gun competition.

American Eagle .223 Tactical is a solid factory choice for most AR-15 users.

Federal American Eagle 55-grain FMJ

Available in 1,000-round bulk packs, Federal's American Eagle 55-grain FMJ is a solid all-around load for 3-gun. While some competitors prefer a heavier bullet for long-range shooting, 55-grain bullets are most likely still the most common bullet weight used.

Loose-packed for added value, this load delivers a muzzle velocity of 3,420 fps. A 1,000-round bulk pack retails for about $370, but can be found marked down online on occasion.

Hornady Steel Match Ammunition

Utilizing coated steel cartridge cases, instead of traditional brass, Hornady Steel Match Ammunition costs as much as 40-percent less than brass cased match ammo. However, Hornady loads these rifle rounds with Match bullets and the pistol loads with HAPs, delivering accurate, yet affordable, ammunition designed specifically for competition.

Steel Match is available in .223 and .308, as well as 9mm, .40 S&W, and .45 ACP. The .308, .40, and .45 loads, though loaded to moderate velocities to reduce recoil, meet IDPA and IPSC/USPSA Major power factor.

Hornady's new Steel Match delivers pistol and rifle ammunition at a reduced cost, with steel cases being less expensive to manufacture than traditional brass.

Remanufactured Ammo

Another way to save money on ammunition is through factory-loaded, remanufactured ammunition. Here, ammo companies acquire spent brass, often through military and law enforcement channels, then re-load it to certain specifications.

Remanufactured ammunitions are most often used as training rounds, with competitors still electing to use match-grade factory ammo for competition. Black Hills, Atlanta Arms & Ammunition, and others offer both pistol and rifle loads suitable for sending a large volume of practice rounds downrange.

(above) Hornady .308 Match is a popular load for Heavy Metal shooters.

(left) Competitors go through a lot of rifle rounds at a major 3-gun match.

(below) Major 3-gun matches are conducted as "lost brass" matches, meaning competitors are prohibited from picking up the empty casings they just fired. A volunteer-driven sport, the lost brass often is given to the range officers and staff, while other ranges sell used brass.